ABRAHAM AND DAVID

STUDIES IN BIBLICAL THEOLOGY

A series of monographs designed to provide clergy and laymen with the best work in biblical scholarship both in this country and abroad

STUDIES IN BIBLICAL THEOLOGY

Second Series · 5

ABRAHAM AND DAVID

Genesis XV and its Meaning
for Israelite Tradition

R. E. CLEMENTS

SCM PRESS LTD

BLOOMSBURY STREET LONDON

FIRST PUBLISHED 1967
© SCM PRESS LTD 1967
PRINTED IN GREAT BRITAIN BY
ROBERT CUNNINGHAM AND SONS LTD
ALVA

CONTENTS

ABBREVIATIONS

AcOr	*Acta Orientalia*
AJSL	*American Journal of Semitic Languages and Literatures*
ANET	*Ancient Near Eastern Texts Relating to the Old Testament*, ed. J. B. Pritchard, 2nd ed., Princeton, 1955
ANVAO	Avhandlinger utgitt av det norske Videnskaps-Akademi i Oslo
ASTI	*Annual of the Swedish Theological Institute*
BA	*The Biblical Archaeologist*
BH	Biblia Hebraica, 3. Aufl., Stuttgart
BHH	*Biblisches-historisches Handwörterbuch*, Göttingen, 1962-7
BJ	La Bible de Jerusalem
BKAT	Biblischer Kommentar: Altes Testament
BRL	*Biblisches Reallexicon*, ed. K. Galling, Tübingen, 1937
BWANT	Beiträge zur Wissenschaft vom Alten und Neuen Testament
BZ	*Biblische Zeitschrift*
BZAW	Beihefte zur Zeitschrift für die alttestamentliche Wissenschaft
CAH	Cambridge Ancient History, revised edition, Cambridge
CBQ	*Catholic Biblical Quarterly*
ET	*Expository Times*
EVV	English versions
FRLANT	Forschungen zur Religion und Literatur des Alten und Neuen Testaments
HKAT	Handkommentar zum Alten Testament
HTR	*Harvard Theological Review*
HUCA	*Hebrew Union College Annual*
IB	*The Interpreter's Bible*, New York—Nashville
ICC	International Critical Commentary, Edinburgh
IDB	*The Interpreter's Dictionary of the Bible*, New York—Nashville, 1962
IEJ	*Israel Exploration Journal*
JBL	*Journal of Biblical Literature*

JBR	*Journal of Bible and Religion*
JCS	*Journal of Cuneiform Studies*
JNES	*Journal of Near Eastern Studies*
JSS	*Journal of Semitic Studies*
KAT	Kommentar zum Alten Testament
LXX	Septuagint
NGT	*Norsk Geografisk Tidsskrift*
NTT	*Norsk Teologisk Tidsskrift*
OLZ	*Orientalistische Literaturzeitung*
OTS	*Oudtestamentische Studiën*
PEQ	*Palestine Exploration Quarterly*
RB	*Revue Biblique*
RGG	*Die Religion in Geschichte und Gegenwart*, Tübingen, ²1927-32, ³1957-63
RHPR	*Revue d'Histoire et de Philosophie Religieuses*
RHR	*Revue de l'Histoire des Religions*
SBT	Studies in Biblical Theology
StTh	*Studia Theologica*
STU	*Schweizerische theologische Umschau*
SVT	*Supplements to Vetus Testamentum*
Syr.	Syriac
ThLZ	*Theologische Literaturzeitung*
VT	*Vetus Testamentum*
WC	Westminster Commentaries
WMANT	Wissenschaftliche Monographien zum Alten und Neuen Testament
WZ Leipzig	*Wissenschaftliche Zeitschrift der Karl Marx Universitet Leipzig*
ZAW	*Zeitschrift für die alttestamentliche Wissenschaft*

I

INTRODUCTION

IN the modern study of the Old Testament the importance of the covenant concept for ancient Israel has been affirmed from a number of directions. The organization of Israel before the establishing of the monarchy as a federation of tribes presupposes some kind of formal covenant structure to its existence, and a historical analogy for such an organization has been found in the early Greek and Italian religious amphictyonies. Further to this the formal pattern evidenced in Israel's own accounts of its covenant with Yahweh has been usefully illuminated by comparison with political treaties of various kinds from the Hittite and Assyrian empires of the second and first millennia BC. From another direction, the significance of covenant forms and ideology has entered into prominence in Old Testament studies in connection with the nature and purpose of Israel's worship. The existence of a covenant between Yahweh and Israel has appeared as a fundamental presupposition of Israelite worship, in which the making of that covenant was recalled and its obligations reaffirmed. Thus the ongoing life of Israel was deeply affected by the recognition of its covenant basis, and both in its religious and political organization the belief in a divine covenant had a central place.

In view of the emphasis which the Old Testament literature places upon the Sinai covenant, in which Moses acted as mediator between God and Israel, it is natural that this should have received most attention from scholars.[1] This was not the only covenant, however, which affected Israel's life. The Davidic dynasty, which maintained a comparatively long period of rule over Judah, was believed also to have been established by a divine covenant made between Yahweh and David (II Sam. 7). The form of this cove-

---

[1] Cf. especially W. Beyerlin, *Origins and History of the Oldest Sinaitic Traditions*, Oxford, 1965, and M. L. Newman, *The People of the Covenant. A Study of Israel from Moses to the Monarchy*, London, 1965.

9

nant is very different from that made on Sinai, and it belonged to
a very different type of socio-political structure from the tribal
federation where the tradition of the Sinai covenant originally
belonged. This undoubtedly gave rise in Israel to a degree of
tension between the specifically Davidic and Sinaitic traditions,
which was not truly overcome until the exilic and post-exilic
periods. Certainly Israel's covenant ideology was not all of one
kind, nor was it entirely focused upon a single person or a single
event. Other covenants besides the Sinaitic made important
contributions to Israel's history and religion, and the various historical and prophetic texts of the Old Testament bear a differing
witness to their relative importance.

Among these various traditions we have preserved a recollection of a covenant made by God with the patriarch Abraham, of
which the book of Genesis gives us two accounts. The older of
these is given in Genesis 15 (J +), and the later in Genesis 17 (P).
A comparison of the two accounts shows that the later one is not
the result of an independent historical tradition, but is the result
of theological reflection upon the earlier narrative. During the
course of Israel's history, with its changing political fortunes, the
need was felt to draw out certain features belonging to the tradition of this Abrahamic covenant, and to provide it with a new
emphasis. This is undoubtedly the reason why the original tradition was represented in a revised form. Many scholars have maintained that the early account in Genesis 15 was never the basis of
any actual religious or political institution of Israel's ancestors,
but was purely a literary and theological development designed to
offer a divine assurance for Israel's possession of its land at a time
when this had become endangered. More recently, under the
stimulus of traditio-historical investigation, an original nucleus of
tradition, which antedated the introduction of the monarchy in
Israel, and which pointed back to a very ancient religious and
political situation has been discerned in Genesis 15. This opens a
useful possibility for reconsidering the tradition of the Abrahamic
covenant, and for investigating afresh the nature of its contribution to the development of Israelite-Jewish religion.

The value of such a study is all the more suggested by the
remarkable paucity of references to Abraham and the divine
covenant with him in Israel's prophetic literature before the exile.
In the JE history, as well as in the introductory sections to the

Code of Deuteronomy, the Abrahamic covenant is given a position of importance, whereas in the pre-exilic prophets it plays no part at all.[2] It is not until we come to the great prophets of the exile, Ezekiel and Deutero-Isaiah, that appeal is made to Abraham as the ancestor who received a divine promise of possession of the land of Canaan. Since this promise is central to the Abrahamic covenant, the reawakened interest in the promise of the land betokens a revived interest in the covenant of which it was a part. How are we to explain this indifference to the Abrahamic covenant in the pre-exilic prophets, and what reasons are we to ascribe to the change that took place during the exile? This strange history of the tradition of the divine covenant with Abraham confirms the need for a careful study of the Old Testament references to it.

Such a study may also make some useful contribution to the many problems concerning the historicity of the Old Testament patriarchal traditions in general, especially since Genesis 15 represents a focal point of the whole Abraham tradition.[3] With the continued amassing of archaeological information from the ancient Near East, a remarkable reappraisal has taken place in regard to the setting of the Hebrew patriarchs in general history. Comparison of the patriarchal narratives with the social customs, racial movements and political history of the ancient Orient, as revealed by archaeology, has brought about a very much more positive and confident evaluation of their authentic historical colouring.[4] This reappraisal is greatly to be welcomed, and although the present study does not attempt to make any further

---

[2] This has been particularly demonstrated by K. Galling, *Die Erwählungstraditionen Israels* (BZAW 48), Giessen, 1928, especially pp. 37ff., 63ff.

[3] G. von Rad, *Genesis*[2], London, 1963, p. 184, calls it 'one of the oldest narratives in the tradition about the patriarchs'.

[4] The literature is now considerable, but the following works may be particularly mentioned: H. H. Rowley, 'Recent Discovery and the Patriarchal Age', *The Servant of the Lord and other Essays on the Old Testament*[2], Oxford, 1965, pp. 281-318; J. Bright, *A History of Israel*, London, 1960, pp. 60ff.; G. E. Wright, *Biblical Archaeology*[2], London, 1962, pp. 40ff.; J. M. Holt, *The Patriarchs of Israel*, Nashville, 1964; R. de Vaux, *Die hebräischen Patriarchen und die modernen Entdeckungen*[2], Düsseldorf, 1961 (translated from *RB* 53, 1946, pp. 321-48; *RB* 55, 1948, pp. 321-47; *RB* 56, 1949, pp. 5-36), and 'Les patriarches hébreux et l'histoire' *RB* 72, 1965, pp. 5-28 (partly translated as 'The Hebrew Patriarchs and History', *Theology Digest* 12, 1964, pp. 227-40); S. Yeivin, 'The Age of the Patriarchs', *Rivista degli Studi Orientali* 38, 1963, pp. 277-302.

contribution towards utilizing the findings of archaeology to illuminate the patriarchal traditions, it does not mean to minimize the results so far attained. The testimony given to the patriarchs by archaeology, for all its substantiality, is indirect, and is concerned primarily with their general environment. For a direct testimony to the patriarchs we must turn to the Old Testament itself, and to the narratives preserved in Genesis. Since these narratives were compiled long after the events, they undoubtedly passed through a long process of oral transmission before reaching their present form. Before we can use these narratives to obtain any useful picture of the history which initiated them we must subject them to careful examination regarding their form, purpose, and the nature of their transmission, as has been ably demonstrated by H. Gunkel.[5] Only in this way can we evaluate properly the direct testimony which the Old Testament gives to the patriarchs.

The neglect of traditio-historical method in some recent attempts to reaffirm the historical basis of the Hebrew patriarchal traditions on the basis of comparative archaeological evidence can only be regarded as mistaken. The unfortunate consequence has been to suggest that archaeological method and traditio-historical study of the Old Testament narratives are rival schools of interpretation.[6] Such need not, and certainly ought not, to be the case. The illumination provided by archaeology may serve as a useful aid to the study of the traditions which have been preserved, whilst at the same time it cannot dispense with the most careful literary and historical study of these traditions. Very tenuous hypotheses have been put forward in order to fit the patriarchs into a known scheme of Near Eastern history, which have sometimes placed too much weight upon secondary elements

[5] H. Gunkel, *Genesis*, (HKAT), Göttingen, 1901. The important introduction to this commentary was translated into English as *The Legends of Genesis*, Chicago, 1901.

[6] The two methods of approach are well exemplified by a comparison of the estimates of the historical significance of the patriarchs in J. Bright's *A History of Israel* and M. Noth's *The History of Israel*[2], London, 1960, pp. 121ff. Cf. also Noth's review of Bright's work in *Interpretation* 15, 1961, pp. 61-66, and G. E. Wright, 'Modern Issues in Biblical Studies. History and the Patriarchs', *ET* 71, 1959/60, pp. 292-6, with the rejoinder by G. von Rad, 'History and the Patriarchs', *ET* 72, 1960/61, pp. 213-6. See also R. de Vaux, 'Method in the Study of Early Hebrew History', *The Bible in Modern Scholarship*, ed. J. P. Hyatt, Nashville, 1965, pp. 15-29, and A. S. Kapelrud, 'Hvem war Abraham?' *NTT* 64, 1963, pp. 163-74.

of the traditions. We must constantly be on our guard against overpressing the significance of the evidence we have, simply because we have it. In itself the employment of comparative evidence from archaeology cannot claim to provide a more objective method of Old Testament research than that provided by traditio-historical study of the narrative material. In all evaluation of the witness of the Old Testament the subjective judgment of the scholar is an inescapable factor, both in comparing it with the evidence of archaeology and in examining the structure of the literary units of which it is composed. The very conflicting conclusions which have been put forward regarding the background and dating of the patriarchs on the basis of archaeological findings may serve as a sufficient proof of this. All our knowledge of the history and culture of the ancient Near East can only serve to clarify the history of the Hebrew patriarchs when it is set in conjunction with a detailed study of the literary witness of the Old Testament, and this inevitably necessitates a consideration of the nature and character of that witness. The evidence of archaeology is subject to limitations which must be understood and respected, and which in no way deny the value of its contribution.[7] A full use of the evidence which it provides must be coupled with the most careful study of the nature, purpose and reliability of the Old Testament traditions which we have.

The aim of this present study is to consider afresh the traditio-historical investigation of the account of a divine covenant with Abraham, since this is central to the whole Abraham tradition, and gave to Abraham a continuing significance for later generations. From the way that the account in Genesis 17 reworked the earlier tradition of Genesis 15 it is apparent that the belief in such a covenant continued to have importance for Israel centuries after the historical situation which gave rise to it had passed away. It is therefore not simply the historical setting of Abraham that we must consider, but also the historical impact of the tradition which grew up around him. In the light of its continuing significance to Israel, Abraham became second in importance only to Moses, who was regarded as a chosen mediator of divine truth, as a typified exemplar of faith and piety.

We may add a further point in justification of the ensuing study.

[7] Cf. M. Noth, 'Der Beitrag der Archäologie zur Geschichte Israels', *SVT* VII, Leiden, 1960, pp. 262-82.

Within both Judaism and Christianity there has grown up a certain contrast between the covenant with Abraham and the covenant of Sinai; the former contained the promises of Israel's election, whilst the latter introduced the demands which this election made in the form of law. This goes back to the presentation of the Abrahamic and Sinaitic covenants in the Old Testament, in the former the element of divine promise predominates, and in the latter the introduction of a law through which obedience to the covenant was to be expressed. It has been suggested that we should make a clear formal distinction between the type of promissory covenant to which that with Abraham belongs, and the type of law covenant, as made with Israel on Mount Sinai.[8] For theological purposes this distinction is of very great significance since it lays bare the fact of a tension between divine promise and divine law, of which both Judaism and Christianity have been conscious in their attempts to provide a theological interpretation of the Old Testament. Thus very different approaches to the Old Testament have emerged according as the idea of 'law' or 'promise' has been given greatest prominence. In our present study it is hoped to clarify this contrast by investigating the historical and institutional factors which exercised a formative influence upon the shaping of the tradition of the Abrahamic covenant. By doing so it may be possible to show the nature of the promise which it contained, and its relationship to later institutions of Israel. Both for theological as well as historical reasons an attempt to reconsider the part played by the Abrahamic covenant in Israel's life may be regarded as justified.

[8] G. E. Mendenhall, 'Covenant Forms in Israelite Tradition', *BA* 17, 1954, pp. 72ff., and 'Covenant' *IDB* I, pp. 717f. Cf. also D. N. Freedman, 'Divine Commitment and Human Obligation. The Covenant Theme', *Interpretation* 18, 1964, pp. 419-31.

II

THE YAHWIST'S ACCOUNT OF THE
ABRAHAMIC COVENANT

THE earliest of the connected histories of the origin and rise of
Israel which the Old Testament contains is that of the Yahwist,
which recent criticism ascribes to the tenth century BC.[1] After an
account of the primeval history of mankind, which was prefixed
to the whole epic, it describes Yahweh's summons to Abraham
to leave his home in Mesopotamia, and to journey to a land which
God would show him:

> Then Yahweh said to Abram, 'Go from your land and your kindred
> and your father's house to the land which I will show you. I will make
> you into a great nation, and I will bless you, and make your name great,
> so that you will become a blessing. I will bless those who bless you, and
> those who curse you I will curse; and in you all the families of the
> earth will acquire blessing.'[2] (Gen. 12.1-3)[3]

Thus we have a threefold promise to the ancestor Abraham,
which becomes a dominant motif of the whole of the Yahwist's
work. It is reiterated at important moments in the subsequent
narrative in order to recall and reaffirm the divine purpose.[4] The
whole of the Yahwist's epic is constructed around this *tria* of
promises, which are fundamental to his view of Israel's origins.[5]

[1] Cf. G. von Rad, *Genesis*, pp. 23, 29. A. Weiser, *Introduction to the Old
Testament*, London, 1961, p. 102.
[2] The use of the niph'al *wᵉnibᵉrᵉkû* is usually taken in a passive sense.
J. Schreiner, 'Segen für die Völker in der Verheissung an die Väter', *BZ* 6,
1962, p. 7, endeavours to bring out the distinctive sense of the niph'al by
translating 'acquire blessing for themselves'.
[3] The verses in Gen. 12.1-3 must be regarded as a free composition by the
Yahwist himself in which he brings to the fore the distinctive themes which
lend significance to the patriarchal age. Cf. H. W. Wolff, 'The Kerygma of
the Yahwist', *Interpretation* 20, 1966, pp. 131ff. W. Zimmerli, 'Promise and
Fulfilment', *Essays on Old Testament Interpretation*, ed. C. Westermann,
London, 1963, pp. 9off.
[4] Cf. Gen. 18.18; 22.18; 26.4; 28.14; Ex. 2.24; 32.13; 33.1; Num. 32.11.
[5] J. Hoftijzer, *Die Verheissungen an die Drei Erzväter*, Leiden, 1956, pp. 52ff.,
regards the entire theme which centres upon these promises as a later intro-

The Yahwist's purpose was to show the divine providence which brought into being the Davidic Kingdom, by which Israel became a nation, and took possession of the land of Canaan. The relevance of this scheme of promise and fulfilment to the emergence of the Davidic-Solomonic empire is apparent, even though the historian did not carry the story of his people up to this era, and concluded originally with a brief statement of the conquest.[6] By using the ancient historical traditions of his people the Yahwist was seeking to interpret the divine significance of his own age, and was endeavouring to make plain the hidden purpose of God that had been manifested through it. The rise of Israel was thus directly related to the promise of God to its ancestors.

It is into this general scheme of promise and fulfilment, centred upon the promises made to Abraham, that the account of a covenant between Yahweh and Abraham is set. This is now preserved in Genesis 15, although the whole of this chapter is certainly not by the Yahwist.[7] The defining of the sources used in

duction into the Pentateuchal tradition, arising at a time when Israel's possession of the land of Canaan had been placed in jeopardy. This places it in the late pre-exilic, or even exilic, periods. A rejection of this view of Hoftijzer's will become apparent in our whole interpretation of Gen. 15, and its relation to the Yahwist's work.

[6] Cf. G. von Rad, 'The Form-Critical Problem of the Hexateuch', *The Problem of the Hexateuch and Other Essays*, Edinburgh, 1966, p. 73, and S. Mowinckel, *Tetrateuch-Pentateuch-Hexateuch. Die Berichte über die Landnahme in den Drei altisraelitischen Geschichtswerken* (BZAW 90), Berlin, 1964, pp. 9ff. Cf. also B. L. Goff, 'The Lost Yahwistic Account of the Conquest of Canaan', *JBL* 53, 1934, pp. 241-9, who argues that the original J account of the conquest has been lost, but that later editors made summaries based on this old J material.

[7] For Genesis 15 the following major studies are to be noted: A. Caquot, 'L' alliance avec Abram (Genèse 15)', *Semitica* 12, 1962, pp. 51-66; H. Cazelles, 'Connexions et structure de Gen. XV', *RB* 69, 1962, pp. 321-49; S. R. Driver, *The Book of Genesis*[12] (WC), London, 1926; W. Eichrodt, *Die Quellen der Genesis von neuem untersucht* (BZAW 31), Giessen, 1916, pp. 62-65; H. Gunkel, *Genesis* (HKAT), Göttingen, 1901; P. Heinisch, *Das Buch Genesis übersetzt und erklärt*, Bonn, 1930; G. Hölscher, *Geschichtschreibung in Israel. Untersuchung zum Jahvisten und Elohisten*, Lund, 1952, pp. 278ff.; S. H. Hooke, 'Genesis', *Peake's Commentary on the Bible*[2], ed. H. H. Rowley and M. Black, Edinburgh, 1963, p. 190; O. Kaiser, 'Traditionsgeschichtliche Untersuchung von Genesis 15', *ZAW* 70, 1958, pp. 107-26; R. Kraetschmar, *Die Bundesvorstellung im A.T. in ihrer geschichtlichen Entwickelung*, Marburg, 1896, pp. 58ff.; M. Noth, *Überlieferungsgeschichte des Pentateuch*, Stuttgart, 1948, pp. 29, 218, 251-2; O. Procksch, *Genesis* (KAT), Leipzig, 1924, G. von Rad; *Genesis*[2], London, 1963; C. A. Simpson, 'Genesis', *IB*, I, 1952, pp. 437-829; J. Skinner, *Genesis*[2] (ICC), Edinburgh, 1930; L. A. Snijders, 'Genesis XV. The Covenant with Abram', *OTS* XII, Leiden, 1958, pp. 261-79; E. A. Speiser, *Genesis* (The

its composition is extremely difficult and fraught with uncertainties, but the view that the basis of the chapter derives from the Yahwist has gained a wide measure of agreement.

Since J. Wellhausen a considerable number of scholars have recognized that a major break occurs between verses 6 and 7, and that we are presented with two separate narratives, only the second of which actually describes Yahweh's promise as a covenant. In the following translation these two sections are treated as separate units, although it must be borne in mind that several scholars have sought to apportion both sections between J and E, whilst others have argued for a dependence of one section upon the other. We begin with a translation of verses 1-6:

> After these things the word of Yahweh came to Abram in a vision,[8] 'Do not fear,[9] Abram, I am your shield;[10] your reward shall be very great.'[11] Then Abram said, 'O Lord Yahweh, what wilt thou give me

Anchor Bible), New York, 1964; R. de Vaux, *La Genèse* (BJ), Paris, 1953; P. Volz and W. Rudolph, *Der Elohist als Erzähler. Ein Irrweg der Pentateuchkritik? An der Genesis erläutert* (BZAW 63), Giessen, 1933, pp. 25-34; J. Wellhausen, *Die Composition des Hexateuchs und der historischen Bücher des A.T.²*, Berlin, 1899, pp. 23f.; H. Seebass, 'Zu Genesis 15', *Wort und Dienst*, N.F. 7, Bethel, 1963, pp. 132-49.

[8] H. Gunkel and many others have taken the term *maḥᵃzēḥ*, which is rare in the Pentateuch (only occurring again in Num. 24.4, 16), as indicative of the E source, which employs the terminology of prophecy with some freedom (cf. Gen. 21.12; 22.1; 46.2). O. Kaiser considers it a sign of a late redaction, but H. Cazelles points out that there is no obvious reason why such a technical expression of the prophetic experience should not have been current in Israel in the eleventh-tenth centuries BC. In itself it provides slender evidence of the use of E, all the more so in that such a source would first appear here in the Pentateuch, and this can hardly have been the commencement of a written document. Cf. P. Volz and W. Rudolph, *op. cit.*, p. 28.

[9] This phrase points to the style of the Priestly *Heilsorakel*, as both Kaiser and Cazelles point out. Cf. J. Begrich, 'Das priesterliche Heilsorakel', *Ges. Stud. zum A.T.*, Munich, 1964, pp. 217-31, and see the Mesopotamian parallels in *ANET²*, p. 451.

[10] The term 'shield' is frequently used as a metaphor expressing divine protection. See Deut. 33.29; II Sam. 22.3, 36; Pss. 3.4 (EVV. 3); 28.7; 33.20; 59.12 (EVV. 11); 84.10, 12 (EVV. 9, 11); 115.9, 10, 11; 119.114; 144.2. It is particularly appropriate to royal status, as is shown by II Sam. 1.21; Pss. 47.10 (EVV.9); 84.10 (EVV.9); 89.19 (EVV.18). O. Kaiser sees this, and the presence of the form of the *Heilsorakel*, as pointing to a royal oracle of assurance connected with the Davidic court. There is no valid support for the view of E. A. Leslie, *Old Testament Religion*, New York, 1936, pp. 67f. that 'shield' here is a divine title, as A. Alt also accepts. Cf. A. Alt, 'The God of the Fathers', *Essays on Old Testament History and Religion*, Oxford, 1966, p. 66.

[11] Kaiser connects the use of the word 'reward' (*śākār*) with the payment of soldiers. Cf. Ezek. 29.19; Isa. 40.10; 62.11. He comments on the oracle as a

since I continue childless,[12] and a servant is my adopted heir?'[13] Then Abram said, 'Look, thou hast given no descendant to me, and an adopted son will be my heir.'[14] Then behold Yahweh's word came to him, 'This man will not be your heir, but your own son shall be your heir.' Then he brought him outside and said, 'Look up to the sky and count the stars, if you are able to do so.' Then he said to him, 'Thus shall your descendants be.' So he believed[15] Yahweh, and he accounted it to him as righteousness.[16] (Gen. 15.1-6)

Aside from the removal of verse 3 as a gloss upon verse 2, there is no reason why this section should not be regarded as a unity, nor why it should not be dated early. The connections with Deuteronomic usage are perfectly explicable as a result of contacts between this section and the Israelite traditions upon which Deuteronomy itself drew. The complicated literary division between J and E, such as H. Gunkel and O. Procksch advocated, may be rejected as far too arbitrary to carry conviction. As

---

whole, 'It was concerned originally with an oracle of assurance to a king to whom Yahweh promises protection in war, victory and great spoil' (*op. cit.*, p. 115). Cf. H. Cazelles, *op. cit.*, p. 328.

[12] Verse 2 is notoriously corrupt and fraught with uncertainties. The rendering 'I continue childless' is not altogether free from difficulty. The participle *hôlēk* (= continue?) is variously interpreted. K. Galling, *Die Erwählungstraditionen Israels*, pp. 45f., sees it as indicative of an original location of the oracle outside of Canaan, and he regards it as a sign that it once concerned Abram's departure to the promised land. Cf. G. von Rad, *Genesis*, p. 179. This is to build too much on an awkward expression. H. Cazelles regards it as a military metaphor, 'going out (to battle)', and then connects *ʿᵃrîrî* (= barren, childless in Lev. 20.20f.; Jer. 22.30) with the Ugaritic *ʿwr* or *ʿrr* in the sense of 'to awaken, stir up'. Since, however, the question of an heir for Abraham is vital to the section as a whole the traditional interpretation of *ʿᵃrîrî* cannot be dispensed with.

[13] This reads *ûben—mešeq ben—bêtî*, and omits *hû dammešeq ʾᵉlîʿezer* as later glosses upon an unfamiliar expression. *mešeq* is to be connected with the Ugaritic *mšq mlkt*, as H. Cazelles, *op. cit.*, pp. 330f., points out, and compared with the *mašqeh* of Gen. 40.2ff. Thus *ben mešeq* = steward. Cf. C. H. Gordon, 'Damascus in Assyrian Sources', *IEJ* 2, 1952, pp. 174f.; M. F. Unger, 'Some Comments on the Text of Gen. 15.2, 3', *JBL* 72, 1953, pp. 49f., and E. A. Speiser, *Genesis*, pp. 111f. This reading has the support of Theodotian, Vulg. and Targ. We must then assume that a second *ben* has dropped out, and take *ben bêtî* as referring to a slave freed by adoption (so H. Cazelles, *op. cit.*, p. 331).

[14] Verse 3 must be regarded as a gloss upon the difficult verse 2 which became corrupted at an early stage.

[15] We may perhaps read here *wayyaʾᵃmēn* with BH³, following the LXX, but the Hebrew text can be retained. Cf. P. Joüon, *Grammaire de l'hébreu biblique*, Rome, 1923, p. 335.

[16] For this expression see G. von Rad, 'Faith Reckoned as Righteousness', *The Problem of the Hexateuch and Other Essays*, Edinburgh, 1966, pp. 125-30.

J. Wellhausen[17] argued, the basic division of Genesis 15 comes between verses 6 and 7. The question remains whether this opening section can be ascribed to E, chiefly on the ground of its prophetic elements, and in spite of the problem posed by the use of the divine name Yahweh. The ascription to E has recently been readvocated by H. Cazelles, but there is much to favour the view of R. de Vaux that it represents a separate, and in part parallel, tradition to that of verses 7ff., without necessarily deriving from E.[18] The question whether this section shows dependence upon verses 7ff., or *vice-versa*, may be considered after we have dealt with the latter verses.

The basic form of Gen. 15.1-6 is that of an oracle of assurance, perhaps suggesting certain royal motifs, in which Abraham is promised a direct heir who will maintain his inheritance. Thus the question dealt with is not simply that of the descendants of Abraham, and their growth in numbers, but with Abraham's inheritance. By this we must assume that the land on which Abraham dwelt was intended, so that this section is concerned with the promise of land as well as of descendants, and thereby connects with verses 7ff.[19] In seeking to analyse the structure and tradition-history of the section it appears that the oldest material is contained in verses 1, 2 and 4, which deal with the immediate question of an heir for Abraham, and that verses 5-6, which relate the oracle to a later political and religious situation, were developed subsequently. At no point is the promise said to have been rooted in a covenant agreement, and no covenant ceremony is described. The original basis of the oracle would seem to have been a divine assurance that Abraham's inheritance would pass to his direct descendants, and not to those who were regarded as born from a slave wife. This points us back to a period of rivalry for land possession between various clan groups who were regarded as descended from Abraham. The development into an assurance that Abraham's descendants would become as numerous as the stars of the sky took place after the rise of the Davidic empire, when Israel became a great international state. Sometime

[17] J. Wellhausen, *Die Composition des Hexateuchs*, pp. 23f. Cf. G. von Rad, *Genesis*, p. 177.

[18] R. de Vaux, *La Genèse*, p. 81, who comments, 'Here this division of sources is uncertain, and the divergences upon which it has been based are sufficiently explained by the juxtaposition of two coherent accounts, originally independent.'   [19] Cf. A. Caquot, *op. cit.*, p. 57.

subsequent to this the tradition was set down in written form and joined with the allied tradition of verses 7ff.

We can now proceed to a translation and analysis of verses 7-21, which, apart from certain expansions, are generally ascribed to the Yahwist:

Then he said to him, 'I am Yahweh[20] who brought you out from Ur of the Chaldeans to give you this land to possess.' But he said, 'O Lord Yahweh, how am I to know that I shall possess it?' Then he said to him, 'Bring me a three-year old[21] heifer, a three-year old she-goat, a three-year old ram, a turtledove and a young pigeon.' He brought him all these, cut them in two, and laid each half over against the other; but he did not cut the birds in two.[22] When birds of prey came down upon the carcasses, Abram drove them away.

As the sun was setting, a deep sleep overcame Abram; and look, a terror and great darkness fell upon him. Then Yahweh said to Abram, 'Know for sure that your descendants will be aliens in a land which does not belong to them; they will become slaves to its inhabitants who will oppress them for four hundred years. Then I will pass sentence on the nation which they serve, and afterwards they shall go out with many possessions. You yourself will go to your ancestors in peace; you will be buried in a good old age. In the fourth generation they will return here, for the wickedness of the Amorites is even yet not complete.'[23]

[20] The use of the formula 'I am Yahweh' points us to an original setting in a cultic celebration in which this formula of divine introduction was employed. Cf. Ex. 20.2 and see W. Zimmerli, 'Ich bin Jahwe', *Gottes Offenbarung. Gesammelte Aufsätze*, Munich, 1963, pp. 11-40. O. Kaiser regards the vocabulary of land possession as pointing to Deuteronomic influence, but it is probable that once again we have here examples of the material upon which Deuteronomy drew for its distinctive vocabulary and outlook.

[21] The Hebrew *meŝulleŝet* is cognate with the Ugaritic *mtltt*, and must be translated as 'three-year old'. Cf. J. Gray, *The KRT Text in the Literature of Ras Shamra. A Social Myth of Ancient Canaan*². Leiden, 1964, pp. 11, 32. Both G. R. Driver (*Canaanite Myths and Legends*, Edinburgh, 1956, p. 29) and H. Cazelles (*op. cit.*, p. 336) take it as meaning 'a third part'.

[22] The ritual of cutting the animals in two must be taken as a form of dramatized curse. Cf. Jer. 34.18f. Numerous Near Eastern parallels to such a ritual have now come to light, confirming its purpose of invoking a punishment upon any breach of the oath. See D. J. Wiseman, 'Abban and Alalaḫ', *JCS* 12, 1958, p. 129; C. F. Jean, *Archives Royales de Mari*, II, 1950, p. 83 (No. 37, 6-14) and the Sefire Inscription in H. Donner and W. Röllig, *Kanaanäische und Aramäische Inschriften*, Wiesbaden, I, 1962, p. 42; II, 1964, pp. 240, 252.

[23] Verses 13-16, which connect the promise of the land to the patriarchs with the sojourn in Egypt and the deliverance of the Exodus, may well be a later insertion as O. Kaiser argues (*op. cit.*, pp. 109, 118). J. Hoftijzer, however, in accepting a late date for the chapter as a whole, regards them as belonging to the basic narrative (*op. cit.*, p. 54). They certainly do not belong

When the sun had set and it became dark, look, a smoking oven and a blazing torch passed between these pieces. On that day Yahweh made a covenant with Abram, saying, 'To your descendants I give this land, from the wadi of Egypt[24] to the great river, the river Euphrates, the land of the Kenites, the Kenizzites, the Kadmonites, the Hittites, the Perizzites, the Rephaim, the Amorites, the Canaanites, the Girgashites and the Jebusites.'[25] (Gen. 15.7-21)

We may conclude from this analysis that, apart from the additions in verses 13-16 and 18c, 20-21, the section is a unity and derives from the Yahwist. We may therefore date it, along with the Yahwist's work as a whole, to the tenth century BC. It describes the promise to Abraham and his descendants of the land of 'the Kenites, the Kenizzites and the Kadmonites', which was undoubtedly in the South of Canaan. A later editor has enlarged this original promise to cover the extent of the Davidic empire, and the territory of all the peoples of Canaan, so that it falls into line with the Yahwist's presentation in which the promise to the patriarch was a foretelling of the rise of the Israelite empire. Although the Yahwist himself employed the tradition of the

---

to the original substance of the promise of the land to Abraham, but there is no reason for thinking that they are very much later than the Yahwist. They expand the original narrative, and are in no way an alternative version of it.

[24] Reading *minnaḥal* instead of *minneḥar*. Cf. I Kings 8.65.

[25] The list of ten peoples constituting the pre-Israelite inhabitants of Canaan is unique, since they are elsewhere limited to six or seven (Ex. 3.8, 17; 23.23; 33.2; 34.11; Num. 13.29; Deut. 7.1; 20.17; Josh. 3.10; 9.1; 11.3; 12.8; 24.11; Judg. 3.5; I Kings 9.20; Ezra 9.1; Neh. 9.8). This is pointed out by L. A. Snijders, who recognizes that the three extra names mentioned in Gen. 15 have a special significance (*op. cit.*, p. 262). These three are those of the Kenites, Kenizzites and Kadmonites, and the probability is that these three names belonged to the earliest stage of the tradition of the Abrahamic covenant. They can hardly be later additions, since a later editor or glossator would undoubtedly have added those names which had become fixed in tradition, not those which were not included in it. They must therefore have become part of the tradition of the Abrahamic covenant by the time that the Yahwist received it. This is further corroborated by the fact that at least two of these three names are particularly linked with the South of Canaan, and in the case of the Kenizzites with Hebron where the Abraham tradition originally belonged. (Caleb was a Kenizzite, Num. 32.12; Josh. 14.6, 14. Cf. Gen. 36.11, 15, 42; Josh. 15.17; Judg. 1.13; 3.9, 11; I Chron. 1.36, 53; 4.13, 15. The Kenites also were active in the South, I Sam. 27.10; 30.29).

We conclude, therefore, that the reference to 'the land of the Kenites, the Kenizzites and the Kadmonites' was the original identification of the land, which a later editor has expanded by inserting 'from the wadi of Egypt to the great river, the river Euphrates'. Either the same or a later editor then added the other seven names of its inhabitants.

covenant within this context he did not introduce his own *tria* of
promises into the substance of the covenant account. Nevertheless
he certainly intended it to point forward to the Israelite empire, so
that the subsequent additions serve to bring out this point. The
original local significance of the Abrahamic covenant was thereby
transformed into a divine promise of the rise of Israel as rulers of
the land of Canaan.

It remains for us to consider the relation of the two sections of
Genesis 15 to each other. G. Hölscher[26] regarded verses 7ff. as an
expansion of verses 1-2, 4-6, whilst more recently O. Kaiser[27] has
argued that verses 1-6 were dependent on verses 7ff. From our
ascription of verses 7ff. to the Yahwist, it is clear that this section
should have priority in the claim to originality. Therefore, we
completely reject Hölscher's view. Is there, however, any strong
support for Kaiser's view? It is difficult to see that there is, since
each section contains material that is quite distinctive. There is
some formal parallelism between them, but not such as to prove
dependence. The first section, although it is concerned with the
land in the form of an inheritance, is developed into a promise of
descendants, whilst the second section concentrates entirely upon
the promise of the land. Only the second section refers to the promise as a covenant. We conclude, therefore, that the two sections
were at one time independent, and arose as variant forms of the
tradition of a promise of land to Abraham's descendants. The second section was incorporated into the Yahwist's work, and the
first section, which had continued to circulate orally, was later combined with it. It is not impossible that the editor who combined
the two was also responsible for adding verses 13-16, 18b and
20-21 to the original account. This can only remain a speculation,
but it is clear that the purpose of the additions was to incorporate
into the substance of the Abrahamic covenant a more detailed
foretelling of Israel's origins. In doing so the purpose of the
Yahwist in using the tradition of the covenant was more fully
brought out.

[26] G. Hölscher, *op. cit.*, pp. 278ff., ascribes vv. 1-2, 4-6 to E; vv. 7-8 to Rp,
and vv. 9-18 to E².   [27] O. Kaiser, *op. cit.*, p. 118.

III

THE HISTORICAL SIGNIFICANCE OF THE ABRAHAMIC COVENANT

WE can now proceed beyond the limits of a purely literary and textual criticism of Genesis 15 to uncover as far as possible the basis of the tradition that lies behind it. Our literary analysis of the text has made it evident that the basic narrative is that of the Yahwist in verses 7-12, 17-18ab, and that the primary feature of the covenant was a promise of land. From a human viewpoint the tradition of the covenant served as a claim of entitlement to land on the part of a clan, or clans, who regarded Abraham as their ancestor. It functioned as a deed of entitlement to the land, asserting a divine authority for the settlement upon it of Abraham's descendants.

This concern of the tradition with land possession is a fact of first importance when we come to evaluate the history which gave rise to it. H. Gunkel,[1] followed more recently by J. Hoftijzer,[2] argued that the tradition of the covenant with Abraham arose at a time when Israel felt that its possession of the land of Canaan was in jeopardy. This was in the late period of the monarchy, or even, as Hoftijzer suggests, during the exile. It arose purely as a literary and theological tradition when Israel sought reassurance for its hold upon Canaan in the face of serious political threats from the Assyrians and Babylonians, and had no relation to any specific institution of Israel. A. Alt,[3] however, has sought to find in the tradition a genuine nucleus which derived originally from pre-Israelite times, and which had a particular relevance for the lives of those who remembered it.

Alt found in this tradition an ancient cultic legend, telling how the God of Abraham, who continued to be reverenced by the patriarch's descendants, had first revealed himself, and who thereafter came to be known as the God (or Shield) of Abraham. He

---

[1] H. Gunkel, 'Abraham', *RGG²*, I, col. 66.
[2] J. Hoftijzer, *op. cit.*, pp. 81ff.   [3] A. Alt, *op. cit.*, pp. 48, 65f.

was the leader-god of a semi-nomadic clan, who promised to his devotees land and numerous progeny in fulfilment of their deepest desires. When later the descendants of this clan were incorporated into Israel this older nomadic deity was identified with Yahweh the national God.

The importance of Alt's interpretation has been widely recognized, especially in connection with his fundamental reconstruction of the nature of the patriarchal religion. The covenant tradition of Genesis 15 is regarded by him as a cultic aetiology of the particular god worshipped by the descendants of Abraham in pre-Yahwistic times. Thus it has great historical value as an indication of this early period of religious development in Canaan. Our own attempt to uncover the original historical significance of the Abrahamic covenant can best proceed by making a critique of Alt's position. In this there are three basic considerations: the original location of the covenant ceremony, the identification of the deity who conferred the covenant, and the historical significance of the Hebrew patriarchs in general. We may first deal with the question of the original location of the covenant ceremony.

In its present literary form no precise geographical location is provided for the tradition, and we must either conclude that such a reference has dropped out, or for some particular reason was never given. A. Alt[4] accepts the latter position, and concludes from it that the deity concerned can hardly have been a local Canaanite numen. Consequently this tradition is unlike the other cultic aetiologies which connect the patriarchs with the local 'Elîm of Canaan.[5] Originally, Alt concludes, it arose outside the settled land where the patriarch himself belonged.[6] The lack of any geographical reference, therefore, leads to far-reaching conclusions. We must question, however, whether the covenant ceremony of Genesis 15 does not belong to one of the sanctuaries of Canaan. O. Kaiser[7] suggests that a reference to the locality was dropped from the tradition when the Abrahamic covenant was associated with the wider covenant basis of Israel, especially at Shechem. This presupposes a later connection with Shechem which has no supporting evidence, and which would raise many

---

[4] *Ibid.*, p. 65.   [5] *Ibid.*, pp. 48ff.
[6] Cf. also the interpretation of K. Galling, *op. cit.*, pp. 45f.; H. Seebass, *op. cit.*, p. 143.   [7] O. Kaiser, *op. cit.*, p. 124.

problems. E. Nielsen[8] accepts that Gen. 15.7ff. may originally have been connected with Mamre-Hebron, whilst verses 1-6 show some affinities with the Jerusalem cult tradition. The fact that no geographical location is present in the tradition of the Abrahamic covenant may, however, have a quite simple explanation. J. Wellhausen[9] argued that the Yahwist intended the connection of Gen. 15.7ff. with Mamre to be clear from the reference in Gen. 13.18: 'And Abram moved his tent, and came and dwelt by the terebinths[10] of Mamre, which are at Hebron. Then he built there an altar to Yahweh.' (Gen. 13.18 J). Since Genesis 14 does not belong to any of the major pentateuchal sources and was later inserted into the Yahwist's work, it is reasonable to conclude that in the original Yahwist epic the narrative of Genesis 15.7ff. followed directly upon the reference of 13.18. The Yahwist then had no need to introduce a further specific reference to the sanctuary where the covenant was established.[11]

If the ceremony of Gen. 15.7ff. was at one time connected with Mamre, as the evidence from the Yahwist would imply, then this is in agreement with our contention that the land promised to Abraham's descendants was originally in the South of Canaan, where Hebron served as a regional centre. Hebron in fact is the focal point of the various traditions associated with Abraham.[12] Once the framework of the narratives, which gives them an orientation towards 'all Israel', is discarded, then the most secure historical basis for the original location of the Abraham traditions points to Mamre-Hebron.[13] It is here that the Yahwist locates a

[8] E. Nielsen, *Shechem. A Traditio-Historical Investigation*[2], Copenhagen, 1959, pp. 342f.

[9] J. Wellhausen, *op. cit.*, p. 24. Cf. also J. Lindblom, 'Theophanies in Holy Places in Hebrew Religion', *HUCA* 32, 1961, p. 95.

[10] Cf. LXX, Syr., and Gen. 12.6; 18.4.

[11] The Book of Jubilees 14.11 places the scene of Gen. 15 in Mamre, although this is probably a general inference from the Genesis narratives.

[12] A. Alt, *op. cit.*, pp. 53f.; H. Gunkel, *RGG*[2], I, cols. 68, *Genesis*, pp. xliv, 146f., 180ff. Cf. also G. E. Wright, *Biblical Archaeology*, p. 47, who states, 'Abram is most closely associated with Mamre, South of Jerusalem'. The original connection of Abraham with Hebron is rejected by M. Noth (*Überlieferungsgeschichte des Pentateuch*, pp. 42, 120), who seeks rather to place Abraham's activity further south in the region of the Negeb, whilst accepting that the various traditions were subsequently collected at Hebron. Noth's position is opposed by A. Jepsen, 'Zur Überlieferung der Vätergestalten', *WZ Leipzig* 3, 1953/54, p. 270.

[13] The connection of Abraham with other shrines: Shechem, Gen. 12.6f.; Bethel, Gen. 12.8; 13.3f.; Beersheba, Gen. 21.33 (all J) represents a secondary

cultic legend describing a theophany to Abraham (Gen. 18.1-16a J), and it is here that the later Priestly narrative recorded a tradition of Abraham's tomb in the Cave of Machpelah (Gen. 23 P). The cycle of stories concerning Abraham and Lot would also seem to presuppose an original setting in the region of Hebron.[14] We may be fairly confident, therefore, in arriving at the conclusion that not only did Mamre once provide the setting of the covenant ceremony recorded in Genesis 15, but also that Hebron was the regional centre of a number of traditions about Abraham. The original land once promised to Abraham's descendants must therefore have been the rich territory around Hebron. We conclude that the basis of the Yahwist's account of the covenant with Abraham was a local cult legend of Mamre, comparable to other legends in the patriarchal tradition which connect the patriarchs with important cult centres in Canaan.

The primacy of this question regarding the original location of the tradition of Genesis 15 is apparent from the fact that Alt uses his conclusion in regard to it to identify the god originally involved as the nomadic deity known as the God of Abraham. We must therefore proceed to examine the identity of the God of the covenant in the light of our conclusions regarding its original setting.

In the Yahwist's account of the covenant with Abraham it is presented as though the deity who initiated it was Yahweh the God of Israel. This agrees with the Yahwist's whole view of Israel's religious history in which Yahweh was regarded as having been worshipped from primeval times.[15] This is an anachronism, however, since it is certain that the use of the name Yahweh was intimately bound up with the Mosaic origin of the religion of Israel. Although the name cannot have been entirely new at this time, it was not previously in widespread use, and was certainly not the normal title for God used by the patriarchal clans.[16] If the Abrahamic covenant does derive from a religio-

---

carrying-over to Abraham of other local traditions at a time when Abraham had been elevated to become the great ancestor of all Israel. Cf. A. Alt, *op. cit.*, p. 54; A. Jepsen, *op. cit.*, pp. 276ff.

[14] M. Noth, *Überlieferungsgeschichte des Pentateuch*, p. 43.   [15] Gen. 4.26 J.

[16] Yahweh was most probably either the title, or perhaps an invocation, used of the ancient god of Sinai. Cf. S. Mowinckel, 'Kades, Sinai og Jahve', *Norsk Geografisk Tidskrift* 9, 1942, pp. 21f., and 'The Name of the God of Moses', *HUCA* 32, 1961, pp. 121ff.; A. Alt, *op. cit.*, p. 7.

political institution of pre-Israelite times, then the deity who was originally concerned in it cannot have been known as Yahweh. It is the Yahwist historian who has identified the original deity as an earlier manifestation of Yahweh, and who, in doing so, has overlaid any reference to his original title. It is important, therefore, to examine what evidence we have as to this god's original title.

A. Alt, in locating Genesis 15 outside Canaan, argues that the god of a nomadic clan can reasonably be expected to have promised his worshippers both land and numerous descendants, since these are the blessings which such people most deeply desired.[17] This judgment, however, must be questioned very seriously. The natural presupposition of a covenant tradition in which a god-promised land to his worshippers is that the land belonged to the deity. This points in the direction of a god of the settled land, rather than to a nomadic deity who had no permanent attachment to special places. The primary concern of the covenant with land possession agrees, therefore, with our contention that the covenant tradition belongs to the settled land, and not outside it. In locating the tradition at Mamre the conclusion we must draw is that it was the ancient god of the shrine at Mamre who was believed to have made the covenant with Abraham. This accords perfectly with the nature of the tradition as an entitlement to land possession. The settlement of the Abraham clan in the territory surrounding Hebron infringed upon the rights of the God of Mamre, who was regarded as the divine possessor and ruler of this land. It is perfectly intelligible, therefore, that the belief should have become established that it was with this god's approval that Abraham's descendants occupied it, and this was given formal expression in the tradition of a covenant between Abraham and the God of the sanctuary of Mamre. The precise title of this deity is not known to us, but it must certainly have been a form of the high-god El, since various local manifestations of this deity are attested in the patriarchal narratives.[18] O. Eissfeldt has suggested that his original title may have been El-Shaddai.[19] This has in its favour the fact that this was undoubtedly

---

[17] A. Alt, *op. cit.*, pp. 65f.

[18] Cf. El-'Elyon at Jerusalem (Gen. 14.17-24); El-Roi at Beer-Lahai-Roi (Gen. 16.13-14 J); El-'Olam at Beersheba (Gen. 21.33 J); El-Bethel at Bethel (Gen. 31.13 E; 35.7 E); El-'Elohe-Israel at Shechem (Gen. 33.20 E).

[19] O. Eissfeldt, 'El and Yahweh', *JSS* 1, 1956, p. 36; 'Genesis', *IDB*, II,

an ancient divine title in use in Canaan,[20] which we cannot otherwise locate at any specific sanctuary. It is also suggested by the
fact that later generations of Israelites did see a close relationship
between Abraham and El-Shaddai.[21] Whilst this can only remain
a conjecture it does have a fair plausibility. We may conclude,
therefore, that the original God who granted a covenant to
Abraham in which he promised the territory around Hebron to
the patriarch and his descendants was the El deity of Mamre,
whose full title may well have been El-Shaddai.

We are led by these conclusions into disagreement with Alt's
hypothesis regarding the original location of the Abrahamic
covenant and the identity of the deity who granted it. At this
point we may enlarge our inquiry into a consideration of the
broader issues regarding Alt's theory of the original religion of
the patriarchs. We must concentrate primarily upon the evidence
of the Old Testament and draw our conclusions from there, since
the comparative material which Alt adduces from the Arabs of
Nabatea and Palmyrene in the Hellenistic-Roman period can only
provide a secondary support. We may note, however, that Alt's
use of this comparative material has been subjected to criticism on
account of the considerable historical and geographical distances
which separated such Arabs from the situation of the Hebrew
patriarchs in Canaan.[22]

There are, as Gunkel[23] argued and as Alt[24] accepted, a number
of narratives in the Old Testament concerning all three patriarchs
which may be classified as cultic legends. Thus Abraham is said
to have built the altar at Mamre and worshipped Yahweh there,[25]

---

p. 376. Cf. also R. de Vaux, *Ancient Israel. Its Life and Institutions*, London,
1951, p. 294.
[20] On this title see W. F. Albright, 'The Names Shaddai and Abram', *JBL*
54, 1935, pp. 182ff.; J. Hehn, *Die biblische und die babylonische Gottesidee. Die
israelitische Gottesauffassung im Lichte der altorientalischen Religionsgeschichte*,
Leipzig, 1913, pp. 265ff.; M. Weippert, 'Erwägungen zur Etymologie des
Gottesnamens 'El Šaddaj', *ZDMG* 111, 1961, pp. 42-62. Albright, following
Friedrich Delitzsch, connects the name with the Akk. *šadû*—'mountain',
which is related to the Hebrew *šādeh*—'field'. Thus the significance would be
'mountain god'. Weippert accepts a connection with *šādeh* in the sense of 'El
of the land'. [21] Gen. 17.1ff.
[22] F. M. Cross, 'Yahweh and the God of the Patriarchs', *HTR* 55, 1962,
p. 231; J. Hoftijzer, *op. cit.*, pp. 90ff.
[23] H. Gunkel, *Genesis*, pp. xvff.; *The Legends of Genesis*, pp. 32ff.
[24] A. Alt, *op. cit.*, pp. 47ff. Cf. also R. de Vaux, *Ancient Israel . . .*, pp. 289ff.
[25] Gen. 13.18 J.

Isaac is credited with the founding of the sanctuary at Beersheba,[26] and Jacob is said to have founded the sanctuary of El-Bethel at Bethel.[27] These legends are undoubtedly cultic aetiologies which present the patriarchs as cult-founders in order to provide an authorization for their descendants to participate in the worship of such sanctuaries.[28] In reality, however, as both Gunkel and Alt agree, the patriarchs did not found these cults, which were already in existence at the time of the settlement of the Hebrew clans in Canaan. They originally concerned forms of the Canaanite god El, as the divine titles which have been preserved show.[29]

Because these cults were certainly not founded by the Hebrew patriarchs Alt concludes that they were linked with the names of the patriarchs by their descendants, and that the patriarchs themselves did not belong to the territory of Canaan.[30] A. Jepsen,[31] who follows Alt's conclusions regarding the nomadic character of the patriarchal religion, associates the patriarchs more directly with the settled land by arguing that they led migrations into it. It is very hard, however, to follow Jepsen in accepting that the patriarchs both founded distinctive cults outside Canaan, and also led migrations into it. If the patriarchs Abraham, Isaac and Jacob were responsible for leading the settlements of their descendants into the agricultural land of Canaan, it would be remarkable if they were also the founders of cults which originated outside that land. Here we come up against the fundamental question in the evaluation of the patriarchal tradition in the Old Testament. Were the patriarchs founders of distinctive cults derived from the nomadic sphere of life, or were they leaders of settlements into the agricultural land of Canaan? On our answer to this there hinges the further question whether they belonged outside the settled land or within it. In order to arrive at an answer to these questions we must first examine the evidence of the argument that the patriarchs were founders of particular cults deriving from the nomadic way of life.[32]

[26] Gen. 26.23ff. J.   [27] Gen. 28.18ff. E; 31.13 E; 33.20 E.
[28] For Abraham's connection with other shrines see p. 25 note 13c.
[29] M. Haran, 'The Religion of the Patriarchs. An Attempt at a Synthesis', *ASTI* IV, Leiden, 1965, pp. 32ff., accepts the association of the patriarchs with these *'Elim*, but seeks to distinguish them from the gods of the Canaanites.
[30] Cf. M. Noth, *The History of Israel*, p. 123, 'If that description is correct the patriarchs as historical personalities did not really belong to Palestine at all but only to its vicinity.'   [31] A. Jepsen, *op. cit.*, pp. 269ff.
[32] Cf. F. M. T. Böhl, 'Das Zeitalter Abrahams' *Der alte Orient* 29, 1930, p.

We have noted already that the traditions which associate the patriarchs with the '*Ēlîm* cults of Canaan cannot be used as evidence of the argument that the patriarchs actually founded these cults. In reality these cults were older than the age of the patriarchs, and were linked with the names of the latter in order to render their worship acceptable to their descendants. We may question, however, whether these cults should be separated entirely from the patriarchs themselves, as Alt argues in claiming that only their descendants participated in such worship. If the patriarchs led migrations into the settled land of Canaan, then it is wholly probable that they themselves introduced their clans to the worship of the local cults already existing there. Thus these cultic aetiologies rest upon an authentic historical nucleus in showing that the patriarchs introduced their followers to worship at the sanctuaries which they found in the land, even though they did not actually establish them. Such legends belong to the general theme of 'the promise of the land' which characterizes the whole patriarchal tradition, since they show how the patriarchs began to worship the gods of the land. The belief that it was not the patriarchs themselves, but their descendants who first adopted these cults rests upon the assumption that the patriarchs are really to be placed outside Canaan rather than within it. Yet this assumption is not proved, and the connection of the patriarchs with the land is more intelligible if they led their followers into it, than if they merely promised it to them from outside. The weight of evidence favours the view that Abraham, Isaac and Jacob were directly associated with the settled land, and that the Old Testament tradition is wholly correct in associating them with the '*Ēlîm* of Canaan.

Therefore we must reconsider the evidence, which has been used to present the patriarchs as the founders of distinctive nomadic cults of their own stemming from the desert period. Apart from the cultic legends which connect the patriarchs with the various local forms of El there are numerous references which refer to the God of Abraham, the God of Isaac, the God of Jacob, and the God of My Father.[33] We are faced with the ques-

---

41, 'Abraham's historical importance for us lies not in the sphere of national history, but in that of the history of religion'. See also B. Gemser, *Vragen rondom de patriarchenreligie*, Groningen, 1958, p. 8.

[33] The God of Abraham: Gen. 24.12, 27, 42, 48; 26.24; 31.42, 53; cf.

tion whether these titles are due to the work of the literary editors who have woven the traditions of the three patriarchs into a connected unity, or whether they rest upon an earlier historical usage. In part it is certain that such titles are the work of the Old Testament editors, since it is they who have arranged the patriarchs into a family history.[34] Originally they were unrelated to each other, and were local heroes of the Hebrew settlement in Canaan.[35] Alt, however, argues that such titles as the God of Abraham and the God of Isaac do reflect on ancient usage among the nomadic clans descended from the patriarchs. Both H. G. May and K. T. Andersen have rather modified this view by concentrating their attention upon the title of the God of My Father, which they argue was distinctive of the pre-Mosaic religion of the Hebrews.[36] Similarly M. Haran has argued that such a title was in use for the household deities who were more personally concerned with their worshippers than the great exalted gods.[37] The basis of Alt's view is that the patriarchs were cult founders of a distinctive kind of nomadic religion associated with their unsettled way of life. Neither May, Andersen nor Haran, however, necessarily presuppose that the patriarchs were actual cult-founders, and belonged outside of the settled land, although Haran argues that the patriarchs did effect a religious transformation.[38]

We have already rejected the view that the patriarchs are to be removed outside Canaan, and there is no firm evidence for believing that the patriarchs were cult-founders in any other sense than that they introduced their followers to participate in the cults which they found in the settled land. This is how the Old Testament tradition presents them, and we have argued that it rests upon a substantial basis of history. Such titles as the God of

---

Gen. 48.15. The God of Abraham and Isaac: Gen. 28.13; 31.42; 32.9. The God of Abraham, the God of Isaac and the God of Jacob: Ex. 3.6, 15; 4.5, cf. Ex. 3.16. The God of My (Your etc.) Father: Gen. 31.5, 29, 42, 53; 43.23; 46.3; 50.17; Ex. 18.4. The God of Your Fathers: Ex. 3.13.

[34] Cf. A. Alt, *op. cit.*, p. 21.

[35] Cf. *Ibid.*, pp. 46f.; H. Gunkel, *RGG*², I, cols. 66f.; O. Eissfeldt, *IDB*, II, p. 379.

[36] H. G. May, 'The God of My Father—a Study of Patriarchal Religion', *JBR* 9, 1941, pp. 155-8, 199-200; 'The Patriarchal Idea of God', *JBL* 60, 1941, pp. 113-28; K. T. Andersen, 'Der Gott meines Vaters', *StTh* 16, 1962, pp. 170-88.

[37] M. Haran, *op. cit.*, pp. 35ff.   [38] *Ibid.*, pp. 43ff.

Abraham, the God of Isaac and the God of Jacob must be regarded as the result of later reflection upon the ancestral worship
of Israel, and cannot be explained as deriving from distinctive
cultic traditions. Their use probably did not first arise with the
literary editors of the Old Testament traditions, since it is perfectly conceivable that they first appeared among the clans which
claimed descent from the patriarchs. They were, however, simply
popular titles for the local gods which were associated with the
names of the patriarchs. Therefore they do not reveal to us a
distinctive religious tradition separate from the local *'Ēlîm* cults
of the land.

It is clear, however, that the patriarchs must have brought a
religion, or religions, of some kind with them when they entered
into the land. Does the title 'the God of My Father' give us some
clue to what this might have been? It is possible that it does,
although the evidence is far from strong. We may note in support
of such a view the popularity among Israelites of proper names
which imply a kinship between men and their God (Abimelech,
Ahimelech, etc.).[39] These names no doubt were derived from
ancient ancestral traditions of name-giving, so that, although they
appear long after the demise of the religious traditions in which
they arose, they may provide us with some evidence as to the
character of this pre-Israelite religion. Besides this it must be
stated that many of the features which Alt and others have
adduced as characteristic of the religion of the Hebrew patriarchs
carry conviction because of the general acceptance of the belief
that in primitive times there was a close integration of religion
with social values and needs. Thus an emphasis upon ties of kinship, and a lack of attachment to fixed sanctuaries, are reasonable
assumptions for the religion of an unsettled group of semi-
nomads.[40] When the patriarchs migrated into Canaan they brought
much of their ancestral religion with them, and this must certainly
have influenced their worship at the shrines that they found in the
land. It is possible, therefore, that the title 'the God of My

[39] Cf. M. Noth, *Die israelitischen Personennamen im Rahmen der gemeinsemitischen
Namengebung* (BWANT III: 10), Stuttgart, 1928, pp. 66ff.

[40] This is particularly prominent in the interpretations of patriarchal religion
made by M. Buber, *The Prophetic Faith*, New York, 1949, pp. 31ff., and
V. Maag, 'MALKÛT JHWH', *SVT* III, Leiden, 1960, pp. 129ff.; 'Der
Hirte Israels—eine Skizze von Wesen und Bedeutung der Väterreligion',
STU 28, 1958, pp. 2ff.

Father' is one consequence of this.[41] The important fact for our study is the conclusion that when the patriarchs migrated into Canaan they began to worship the gods which they found established at the sanctuaries in the land.

We arrive at the conclusion that the religion of the Hebrew patriarchs, Abraham, Isaac and Jacob, was primarily the worship of the local manifestations of El which were established in the territory which they occupied. This is the position which was advocated by H. Gressman[42] and R. Kittel,[43] and has found its strongest supporter in recent times in F. M. Cross.[44] It has in its favour the witness of the Old Testament itself, which is our primary source, and, although the traditions attesting it derive from a much later age than that of the patriarchs and are aetiological in form, they do contain information of historical worth. This general conclusion regarding the nature of the religion of the Hebrew patriarchs is wholly consonant with our specific conclusions regarding the origin of the tradition of a covenant with Abraham recorded in Genesis 15. This was a local cult legend of Mamre designed to show how the god of the sanctuary there had made an oath to Abraham entitling him and his descendants to dwell upon the land. The god concerned must originally have been a form of the god El, and may very well have been known as El-Shaddai. This tradition was preserved among the clan, and later clans, which regarded Abraham as their ancestor, and who frequented the sanctuary of Mamre. It was taken up by the Yahwist and woven into his presentation of the patriarchal era as an age of promise, which presaged the rise of Israel as a great national power.

The question remains whether the covenant was originally understood solely in terms of unconditional promise in which no specific obligation was placed upon Abraham. Since there are no stipulations mentioned there is no reason to connect any law code with the covenant. It is difficult, however, to believe that a claim

[41] M. Haran, *op. cit.*, p. 39, regards the patriarchal religion as comprised of elements of the cults of *'Ēlīm*, especially El-Shaddai, the God of My Father and a pre-Mosaic form of Yahweh.

[42] H. Gressmann, *Mose und seine Zeit. Ein Kommentar zu den Mose-Sagen* (FRLANT 18), Göttingen, 1913, pp. 425ff.; 'Sage und Geschichte in den Patriarchenerzählungen', *ZAW* 30, 1910, p. 28.

[43] R. Kittel, *Die Religion des Volkes Israel*, Leipzig, 1921, pp. 27ff.

[44] F. M. Cross, *op. cit.*, p. 235.

on the part of Abraham's descendants that their land had been
divinely given to them should not have been thought to carry with
it certain responsibilities.[45] Predominantly the covenant must have
mentioned an obligation on the part of Abraham's descendants to
remain loyal to the god of Mamre, and to offer to him their worship.
Since the settled land was uppermost in the idea of the covenant,
the tithes of the produce of this land and the firstborn of the
flocks and herds which its inhabitants possessed would have
provided the offerings of this worship.[46] The Yahwist, in his
literary presentation of the Abrahamic covenant, was concerned
for reasons of his own to heighten the emphasis upon the divine
promise, so that it is understandable that any reference to this
obligation of loyalty should have been dropped.

Therefore the Abrahamic covenant was centred originally upon
a divine promise of land possession, but it was not wholly unconditional. In referring this covenant to the political and
religious situation of his own age the Yahwist reinforced its
promissory character by omitting any reference to the correspond-
ing obligations which it entailed. From being a local institution it
was transformed into a promise of Israel's future greatness. We
may now turn our attention to a consideration of the circumstances in which the tradition was handed down to the age of the
Yahwist.

[45] The ritual of Gen. 15.7ff. was a type of curse ritual in which the con-
tracting parties invoked punishments upon themselves in the event of any
breach of the covenant. This becomes plain from Jer. 34.18f. It is remarkable
that in Gen. 15.17 it is the deity, represented by the symbols of a smoking
oven and a blazing torch, who passed between the parts, as though he were
invoking the curse upon himself. There is no indication that Abraham also
passed through the divided pieces so that both parties bound themselves
under this fearful oath. We must either conclude that in the development of
the tradition a serious change was made in which the ritual curse was carried
over from the human to the divine partner, or that the original curse significance of the rite has been weakened into that of a solemn oath.

[46] Cf. the obligation of Jacob to offer tithes to El-Bethel at Bethel (Gen.
28.22), and Abraham's gift of tithes to El-'Elyon at Jerusalem (Gen. 14.20).

IV

THE TRANSMISSION OF THE TRADITION

WE come now to inquire how the tradition of a covenant with Abraham came to be included among the broader religious and historical traditions of Israel's origins, and to ask why it was taken up and elaborated by the Yahwist in such a distinctive way. What impulses gave rise to the belief that Abraham was the ancestor of all Israel, and to the idea that the divine promise of the land to him foretold the rise of the Davidic empire? For a considerable period the tradition must have been handed on orally, and there is no obvious reason why it should have been written down at all before the Yahwist included it in his epic. The question of the nature and reliability of oral tradition has frequently been raised in recent years in connection with the origins of the Old Testament literature, and has given rise to quite diverse conclusions.[1] The parallels which have been adduced from later religious movements, both in Judaism and Islam, may be quite misleading since in these later situations there was undoubtedly present a strong religious motive for the preservation of a received sacred text. This kind of religious motive may well have affected the oral preservation of the prophetic literature in Israel, but was certainly not influential in the early patriarchal age. Some useful comparative evidence for the role of oral tradition in ancient societies may be found in modern pre-literate cultures, even though these are historically

[1] Very positive conclusions have been drawn by E. Nielsen, *Oral Tradition. A Modern Problem in O.T. Introduction* (SBT 11), London, 1954. More critical estimates are offered by J. van der Ploeg, 'Le rôle de la tradition orale dans la transmission du texte de l'Ancien Testament', *RB* 54, 1947, pp. 5-41; G. Widengren, 'Oral Tradition and Written Literature among the Hebrews in the Light of Arabic Evidence, with Special Regard to Prose Narratives', *Ac Or* 23, 1959, pp. 201-62; R. C. Culley, 'An Approach to the Problem of Oral Tradition', *VT* 13, 1963, pp. 113-25; G. W. Ahlström, 'Oral and Written Transmission: Some Considerations', *HTR* 59, 1966, pp. 69-81. Valuable studies are also given by S. Mowinckel in the articles 'Legend', *IDB*, III, pp. 108-10, and 'Tradition, Oral' *IDB*, IV, pp. 683-5. See also E. Jacob, 'Sagen und Legenden II. Im A.T.', *RGG³*, V, cols. 1302-8.

and geographically far removed from ancient Israel.[2] It is apparent that the function of oral traditions must be properly understood, since we cannot assume as a basic motive the desire to record history for its own sake. It is necessary to know the group and institution in which the tradition has been preserved, and the purpose which its preservation was intended to serve, for its historical significance to be evaluated.

The initial motive for remembering the tradition of a covenant between Abraham and the god of Mamre is clear enough since it provided a sanction and entitlement for Abraham's clan to dwell upon the territory surrounding Mamre. The exact extent of the land was only generally defined, and in the first place the clan to whom it applied bore the name of Abraham himself. During the period in which this covenant with Abraham was remembered orally, however, very considerable religious and political changes took place in the region of Hebron, and by the time the Yahwist came to write down his account of it the Abraham clan had long since disappeared as a historical entity. It requires a very careful historical reconstruction, therefore, to attempt to trace the history of the Abrahamic covenant during the period of its oral transmission in the light of the evidence which is available to us.

In this connection the basic methodological approach of tradition-history has been to presume a continuing link between the tradition and the locality with which it was associated. This principle of *Ortsgebundenheit* has proved immensely valuable in elucidating many of the early traditions of Israel, although it has not passed without criticism.[3] Clearly traditions were remembered by people and not by impersonal places or sanctuaries, and whole clans could move their settlements. Nevertheless since elements in the traditions were often connected with geographical features, the continued repetition of the tradition in relation to these features can be reasonably assumed. This particularly applies to where a geographical feature or a particular location were integral parts of the tradition. In our present case the tradition concerns an entitlement to a certain area of land so that we are justified in claiming that it was remembered by those who continued to

---

[2] Cf. J. Vansina, *Oral Tradition. A Study in Historical Methodology*, London 1965.

[3] Cf. especially J. Bright, *Early Israel in Recent History Writing* (SBT 19), London, 1956, pp. 100ff.

occupy this land. It was especially connected with the sanctuary at Mamre, where the cultic ceremony establishing the covenant took place.[4] The primary task therefore is to trace the history of clan settlements in Hebron since the people who inhabited the land were undoubtedly those who had most reason for remembering their divine entitlement to it.

This method, which we have argued is basically sound, has been followed by A. Jepsen in his stimulating study of the history of the patriarchal traditions,[5] and it will be useful to summarize briefly his conclusions. The Old Testament contains ample evidence that in the early period of the Israelite settlement in Canaan the land surrounding Hebron was occupied by the clan of Caleb,[6] and in the pentateuchal traditions there is preserved an account of Caleb's role as a spy, during the period spent in the wilderness, which points to this occupation.[7] M. Noth[8] has convincingly argued that the basic motive of this tradition of Caleb's faith and courage as a spy was to show the particular favour of Yahweh which entitled the Calebites to possess the rich land around Hebron. This tradition also, therefore, was an entitlement to land possession, and was concerned with roughly the same territory as the tradition of the Abrahamic covenant. Jepsen concludes that it was the Calebites who introduced the tradition of the Abrahamic covenant into Hebron, and that Abraham was an ancestor of Caleb.[9] He seeks to harmonize the two traditions in the following way: Abraham led a settlement of his clan into the area of Hebron, but was unable to maintain a permanent hold there. At this time there was a continuing pressure of semi-nomadic groups moving into the cultivated lands in the South of Canaan. Subsequently, under the leadership of Caleb, some descendants of the earlier Abraham clan managed to conquer Kiriath Arba (Hebron) and to expel its inhabitants. By doing so

[4] Cf. M. Noth, *The History of Israel*, p. 122, 'It follows that information about the patriarchs survived and was handed down in connection with the sacred objects established by them (altars or massebahs) at the holy places in question.'

[5] A. Jepsen, *op. cit.*, pp. 271ff. Cf. also A. Weiser, 'Abraham', *RGG*[3], I, cols. 68ff., who follows Jepsen closely.

[6] Josh. 15.13ff. [7] Num. 13-14.

[8] M. Noth, *Überlieferungsgeschichte des Pentateuch*, pp. 143ff.; *The History of Israel*, p. 76.

[9] This possibility is also raised by A. Alt (*op. cit.* p. 53), who concludes that the God of Mamre was not worshipped by Calebites alone.

these Calebites planted the Abraham tradition in the region of Mamre, and claimed that the land which they occupied had been promised to them by a covenant made with their ancestor. A. Jepsen follows Alt in arguing that this covenant was made between Abraham and 'the God of Abraham', the nomadic deity whose cult had been founded by the patriarch. Caleb was thus the leader of the most important thrust into the South of Canaan on the part of the Hebrew clans which later became part of Israel. The Calebite clan subsequently united with other southern clans to form a federation of tribes centred at Hebron, thus giving rise to the city's new name (*Ḥebrôn* = league, covenant place). These southern clans eventually formed the great tribe of Judah which, under David, accepted Yahweh as its God and joined with Israel. It was at this time, when the southern clans adopted Yahwism, that the tradition arose that Caleb had been a loyal Yahwist who had shown exemplary courage and faith in his God.

Jepsen's presentation argues that the Calebite clan was the primary claimant to the Abrahamic covenant tradition, and that through this group it passed into the wider possession of Judah, and thus to all Israel under David.[10] In this way the rise in the estimate of Abraham which made him the great ancestor of all Israel is readily explicable. M. Noth[11] also argues that it was through Hebron, to which the Abraham traditions were brought when it became the centre of the southern federation of tribes, that the various legends about the patriarch became the possession of Judah, and, through this tribe, of all Israel.

It is clear that Jepsen's view is based firmly on the principle of *Ortsgebundenheit*. There is, however, a very serious objection that must be raised against it. Why should the clan of Caleb have produced two very different traditions dealing with the divine gift to them of their land? One urged that it had been promised to them as descendants of Abraham, and the other that it had been promised to their ancestor Caleb by Moses as a reward for his exemplary loyalty to Yahweh. This objection is inseparably bound up with another. The underlying motive of the spy tradition of Num. 13-14 is that Caleb was promised the territory of Hebron because he had shown exceptional faith in Yahweh. Yet according to Jepsen's view Caleb never even worshipped Yahweh, but

---

[10] Cf. also A. Alt, *op. cit.*, p. 54.
[11] M. Noth, *Überlieferungsgeschichte des Pentateuch*, pp. 43, 144.

the God of Abraham, and it was not until the time of David that the Calebite clan was converted to Yahwism. On Jepsen's view the two traditions entitling the Calebites to possession of the Hebron territory represent two eras in their religious history: the promise to Abraham stemming from the time between Caleb's conquest and the rise of David, and the Mosaic promise to Caleb coming from the post-Davidic age when Yahweh became the God of Judah. This is extremely improbable, and the evidence points rather to the conclusion that the two fundamental presuppositions of the spy tradition of Num. 13-14 were that the Calebites occupied the rich lands of Hebron, and that Caleb himself was known to have been a Yahweh worshipper. In fact the conclusion seems inescapable that Caleb not only led a conquest into the region of Hebron, but was responsible for introducing the worship of Yahweh there.[12] Thus when a tribal federation emerged with its centre at the sanctuary of Mamre its God was certainly Yahweh.[13] It is impossible, therefore, that the Calebites could have been responsible for introducing into Hebron the tradition of a divine covenant with Abraham, whether this was in the name of the nomadic God of Abraham, as Jepsen supposes, or the El deity of Mamre, as we have argued.

We must conclude, therefore, that the evidence is against the view that the Calebites were responsible for introducing the tradition of Abraham into Mamre.[14] It is far more likely that this tradition had already been established there when Caleb conquered it. Under Caleb the earlier belief that the god of Mamre had made a covenant with Abraham and his descendants, which entitled them to dwell on his land, gave place to a new tradition giving to the Calebite settlers a special claim to the territory through the belief in a promise made by Moses. Thus the differing land-possession traditions reflected both the changing circumstances in the settlement of the Hebron district, and the changing religious development in which Yahweh supplanted the older god of Mamre.

[12] Thus the achievements of Caleb in the South are in some measure parallel to those of Joshua in the central highlands. Cf. M. Noth, *The History of Israel*, pp. 76f.
[13] Cf. M. Noth, *Überlieferungsgeschichte des Pentateuch*, p. 146 note, 'The covenant cult of Mamre was certainly directed to Yahweh, and at the time of the existence of this covenant the Calebites were also Yahweh worshippers.'
[14] Cf. A. Alt, *op. cit.*, p. 53.

In order to understand the place of the Abrahamic covenant tradition in Hebron, we must consider the evidence we possess for the history of Hebron during the period of the earliest Israelite settlements. This history is by no means fully known, but at least there is sufficient evidence to show that a surprising variety of influences affected it, representing different political and racial interests.[15]

The sanctuary of Mamre was situated a little to the north of Hebron itself, and, as the tradition recalls, was famous for its sacred terebinth trees.[16] The Old Testament preserves a recollection of the founding of Hebron in Num. 13.22b: 'Hebron was built seven years before Zoan in Egypt' (Num. 13.22b JE). The significance of this parenthetic note is not wholly clear. S. Mowinckel[17] regards it as a fragment of a genuinely ancient tradition which recalled an original association between Hebron and Zoan-Tanis, which was identical with the Hyksos capital of Avaris in Egypt. This association could only have been made by the Hyksos themselves, and Mowinckel concludes that Hebron was founded by the Hyksos rulers of Egypt during the fourteenth century BC as the chief fortress by which Egyptian control was to be maintained over the Judaean range of mountains in the South of Palestine. Thus it became a seat of the Hyksos rulers of Egypt, and a military fortress of their power in Palestine. Its original name, however, was not Hebron but Kiriath Arba,[18] which Mowinckel derives from the particular layout of the city, which would have been divided into four quarters. The Old Testament, however, derives it mistakenly from the supposed personal name of a certain Arba.[19]

H. H. Rowley,[20] however, interprets Num. 13.22b as implying

[15] For the history of Hebron cf. K. Elliger, 'Hebron', *BHH*, II, cols. 669f.; V. R. Gold, 'Hebron', *IDB*, I, pp. 575ff.; K. Galling, 'Hebron (und Mamre)', *BRL*, cols. 275ff. A. Kuschke, 'Hebron', *RGG*³, III, col. 110.

[16] Gen. 12.6 J; 13.18 J; 18.4 J. For the archaeology of Mamre cf. especially R. de Vaux, 'Mambré', *Supplément au dictionnaire de la Bible*, V, ed. H. Cazelles, Paris, 1957, cols. 753-8. C. F. Arden-Close, 'The Cave of Machpelah', *PEQ* 83, 1951, pp. 69ff. K. Elliger, 'Mamre', *BHH*, II, cols. 1135f.

[17] S. Mowinckel, 'Die Gründung von Hebron', *Donum Natalicium H.S. Nyberg Oblatum*, Uppsala, 1954, pp. 185ff.

[18] Gen. 23.2; 35.27; Josh. 14.14; 15.13, 54; 20.7; 21.11; Judg. 1.10; Neh. 11.25.

[19] Josh. 14.15.

[20] H. H. Rowley, *From Joseph to Joshua*, p. 76, following F. V. Winnett, 'The Founding of Hebron', *Bulletin of the Canadian Society of Biblical Studies*,

that Caleb captured Hebron seven years before the rebuilding of Avaris—Tanis by Israelite forced labour for Rameses II. Thus the building of both cities is related to Israelite history, and not to the period of Hyksos domination. Rowley finds in this verse supporting evidence for the belief that Hebron was captured by Caleb whilst the tribes that Moses led out of Egypt were still in bondage. We shall see that there is much which points to a settlement of a group of Yahweh worshippers in Judah apart from the main thrust under Joshua, and the placing of this southern movement earlier than that in the centre and the North. It is very questionable, however, whether this view can derive support from Num. 13.22 since this verse is explicitly concerned with the building of Hebron and not its capture. The reference to Zoan is more likely to be connected with the foundation of the city, and thus with its cultural origin, than with its rebuilding by Israelite forced labour. In the case of Hebron we have no reason for ascribing to Caleb any substantial rebuilding of the city. Probability therefore would seem to favour Mowinckel's view that the significance of this evidence lies in its recollection of a cultural and political connection between Hebron and Zoan under Hyksos influence.[21] Thus we can find in Num. 13.22b a fragment of tradition which testifies that Hebron was an Egyptian fortress city established in the fourteenth century BC.

From this century a number of Amarna letters refer to a certain Shuwardata, who was a local prince in the hill country to the South of Palestine,[22] and whose rule may well have extended over Hebron.[23] This Shuwardata was a vassal of the Egyptian Pharaoh, although there is evidence for an episode of disloyalty to this Egyptian suzerainty. He complains in one of his letters to his overlord of attacks made by the SA-GAZ, who are invading settlers akin to the Habiru.

The traditions of the Israelite conquest recall that three clans of

No. 3, June, 1937, pp. 21-29. I am indebted to Professor Rowley for making a copy of Winnett's article available to me.

21 For Hyksos influence upon Canaan during the period of the Israelite settlement cf. A. Alt, 'The Settlement of the Israelites in Palestine', *Essays on O.T. History and Religion*, Oxford, 1966, pp. 139ff., and K. Galling, 'Hyksosherrschaft und Hyksoskultur', *ZDPV* 62, 1939, pp. 89ff.

22 Cf. J. A. Knudtzon, *Die El-Amarna-Tafeln mit Einleitung und Erlauterungen*, Leipzig, 1915, Vol. I, pp. 834ff., 844ff., Vol. II, pp. 1329ff.

23 Cf. *ANET*², pp. 486ff.

Anakim originally dwelt in Kiriath Arba; Sheshai, Ahiman and Talmai.[24] The ascription of the victory over these pre-Israelite clans is variously placed in the Old Testament sources between Joshua, Caleb and the tribe of Judah.[25] V. R. Gold has suggested that there was an initial conquest under Joshua, and a subsequent recapture of Hebron under Caleb.[26] This, however, is very improbable, and the likelihood is that there was an original settlement of Yahweh worshippers in the South of Canaan led by Caleb, whilst Joshua's conquest was restricted to the central highlands.[27] In the development of Israelite tradition the role of Joshua, as the successor of Moses, became greatly enlarged and the complete conquest of Canaan was ascribed to him. Certainly the fact that Caleb was a less illustrious person in Israelite tradition greatly favours the view that the account which ascribes to him the conquest of Kiriath Arba is historically the most reliable. This is particularly so when considered in the light of the non-Israelite origin of the Calebites. Later Israelite tradition would certainly not have ascribed to Caleb an important victory if the historical evidence had not testified to it very strongly. We may conclude, therefore, that it was Caleb who expelled the three clans of the Anakim from the city. When subsequently the Calebites were incorporated into the federation of clans which made up the great tribe of Judah, Caleb's victory was included among the traditions which celebrated the achievements of this tribe. Finally, when the whole conquest of Canaan was ascribed by a united Israel to a single invasion led by Joshua, then the conquest of Hebron was credited to Joshua.

There is every reason to accept the authenticity of the tradition which claims that the Calebites were Yahweh worshippers at the time that they conquered Hebron, and that they were responsible for introducing the cult of Yahweh into the city. The origins of this worship of Yahweh by the Calebites must be traced back to the North Sinaitic peninsula, to the region of Kadesh. H. H.

---

[24] Num. 13.22; Judg. 1.10. E. C. B. MacLaurin, 'Anak/Ἄναξ', *VT* 15, 1965, pp. 468ff. regards Anak as a Philistine title of rank.
[25] Josh. 10.36-39; 11.21-22 ascribes it to Joshua; Josh. 14.13ff.; 15.13ff. ascribes it to Caleb; Judg. 1.10, 19-20 claims the victory for the tribe of Judah.
[26] V. R. Gold, *IDB*, I, p. 576.
[27] H. H. Rowley, *From Joseph to Joshua*, pp. 76f. O. Eissfeldt, *Palestine in the Time of the Nineteenth Dynasty* (a) *The Exodus and the Wanderings* (CAH II: 26(a)), Cambridge, 1965, p. 24.

Rowley[28] ascribes to this Southern (Calebite) movement the responsibility for the introduction of the tradition of a stay at Kadesh into the Israelite account of the nation's origins. This is not impossible, although there is much to suggest that Kadesh was central to the whole tradition of Yahweh worship, so that both the Southern and Northern movements into Palestine, associated respectively with Caleb and Joshua, had an original link with this place. There are indications that Kadesh was the centre of the cult of Yahweh, who was venerated in pre-Israelite times as the God of Sinai-Horeb.[29] Thus it is perfectly credible that both movements, even though separated by a considerable interval of time, should have had connections with Mount Sinai through their common links with Kadesh. Only the later (Northern) movement, however, which entered Canaan under Joshua, had experienced the Exodus from Egypt and enjoyed the leadership of Moses. When these separate elements were united together later through their common religious interests, then the Exodus-Moses traditions were accepted by all. It was at this stage that Caleb's possession of the land of Hebron was especially linked with a promise of Moses giving the land to Caleb as a reward for his courage as a spy.

So far as the date of the conquest of Hebron by Caleb is concerned we must be content with considerable uncertainty. H. H. Rowley[30] places it in the Amarna age, whilst he dates the conquest under Joshua roughly a century later, in the second half of the thirteenth century BC.

In Hebron the Calebites united with a number of other clans to form what has often been regarded as a six-tribe federation.[31] This was made up of the tribes (or clans) of Judah, Caleb, Simeon, Jerahmeel, Cain and Othniel. At some stage the older name of Kiriath Arba gave way to the new name of Hebron, signifying the city's role as the centre for a federation of clans. The God of this Southern federation was Yahweh, for whom the shrine at Mamre served as the most important centre in the South of Canaan. This

[28] H. H. Rowley, *From Joseph to Joshua*, pp. 104ff.
[29] Cf. S. Mowinckel, *NGT* 9, pp. 21ff.; J. Gray, 'The Desert Sojourn of the Hebrews and the Sinai–Horeb Tradition', *VT* 4, 1954, pp. 148-54; W. Beyerlin, *Origins and History of the Oldest Sinaitic Traditions*, pp. 145ff.
[30] H. H. Rowley, *From Joseph to Joshua*, pp. 140ff.
[31] M. Noth, *Das System der Zwölf Stämme Israels* (BWANT IV: 1), Stuttgart, 1930, pp. 107ff.; *The History of Israel*, pp. 181f.

Southern federation ultimately came to comprise 'the House of Judah', which became the title of the whole union, through the domination of this one tribe. Thus the Calebites came to be reckoned to Judah in later Israelite tradition.[32]

The origins of this great tribe of Judah are shrouded in some obscurity. The name itself is probably a geographical one, as M. Noth contends,[33] originally applying to the Southern mountain range and then to the inhabitants who lived upon it. Among its clans there were to be found elements which were never fully integrated into Israel, and T. H. Robinson has gone so far as to argue that it was basically of Canaanite origin.[34] In more recent years a number of scholars have disputed M. Noth's contention that Judah was a member of the pre-monarchic Israel federation, arguing that this was originally a ten-tribe union, which only expanded into a twelve-tribe union under David.[35] The major support for this view has been found in the lack of reference to the tribes of Judah and Simeon in the Song of Deborah. We have already noted that A. Jepsen, in his study of the history through which the patriarchal traditions passed, accepted that Judah did not belong to the Israel federation, nor worship Yahweh, until the time of David.[36] This latter contention, however, we have rejected, although we have found reason to accept that the Southern tradition of Yahwism differed from that practised in the North. The tradition of Moses, and of the conclusion of a covenant on Mount Horeb-Sinai belonged at first to the North, and to those Israelites who had entered Canaan under Joshua. The extent of the union existing between the Southern and the Northern groups of Yahweh worshippers in Canaan before the

[32] Josh. 15.13; cf. Judg. 1.10.

[33] M. Noth, *The History of Israel*, p. 56.

[34] T. H. Robinson, 'The Origin of the Tribe of Judah', *Amicitiae Corolla* (*Rendel Harris Festschrift*), London, 1933, pp. 265-73; *A History of Israel*, Vol. I, Oxford, 1932, pp. 169f. A Canaanite element in Judah seems to be implied by the narrative of Gen. 38. H. H. Rowley accepts that whilst Judah was of mixed origin it contained genuinely Israelite elements (*From Joseph to Joshua*, pp. 5-6 note).

[35] S. Mowinckel, *Zur Frage nach dokumentarischen Quellen in Josua 13-19* (ANVAO 1946: 1), Oslo, 1946, pp. 20ff.; K. D. Schunck, *Benjamin. Untersuchung zur Entstehung und Geschichte eines israelitischen Stammes* (BZAW 86), Berlin, 1963, p. 53. B. D. Rahtjen, 'Philistine and Hebrew Amphictyonies', *JNES* 24, 1965, pp. 100ff., denies that the number twelve was in any way basic to the structure of the Israelite amphictyony, or of other such federations of tribes. [36] A. Jepsen, *op. cit.*, pp. 272ff.

rise of David is very difficult to ascertain. Undoubtedly these links did exist, and the common religious background must have been a major factor in forging them. At some period the differing elements of tradition began to be woven together, and the scheme was created which made the various local patriarchs into succeeding generations of one family. Whilst our knowledge of this elaboration of tradition derives from the post-Davidic age there is no reason to doubt that when the Yahwist took it up it had already gained a wide popular acceptance. Yet even whilst accepting some measure of relationship between Judah and Israel before David's time, we must acknowledge that the political situation which existed in Canaan, coupled with significant geographical factors, imposed severe limitations upon the degree of unity which could be attained.[37]

In rejecting Jepsen's view that the Calebites introduced the tradition of the Abrahamic covenant into Hebron, we have been led to look for this development in a time prior to the Calebite conquest. This means that it was prior to the Amarna period, although we have not been able to give a more precise date than this. Under the Calebites the ancient tradition preserved in Mamre that the deity worshipped there had made a covenant with Abraham was supplanted by the cult of Yahweh and the belief that the land surrounding Hebron had been promised to the Calebites by Yahweh. This was eventually developed into the belief that Caleb had been associated with Moses, who had allocated the land to him at Yahweh's command. These religious developments did not destroy the recollection of Abraham, and the divine covenant with him. Rather this tradition lived on among the new inhabitants who came to regard Abraham as their ancestor.[38] Thus the federation of tribes which had its religious focus in the sanctuary of Mamre came to look back upon Abraham as its great forebear, and this belief became a significant part of the religious heritage of the great tribe of Judah. In this way the

[37] Cf. H. H. Rowley, *From Joseph to Joshua*, pp. 102f.; S. Herrmann, 'Das Werden Israels', *ThLZ* 87, 1962, cols. 568ff.

[38] It is possible that the close link between Abraham and Hebron is reflected in the victory list of the Egyptian Pharaoh Sheshonk I from the tenth century BC. Among the list of places conquered in Canaan there is a mention of 'the fields of Abraham', by which Hebron must be intended. The reading, however, is uncertain. Cf. *ANET*², p. 242, and see J. H. Breasted, 'The Earliest Occurrence of the Name of Abram', *AJSL* 21, 1904/5, pp. 22-36.

ancient belief in Abraham's divinely given inheritance in Hebron continued to be preserved long after it had become obsolete in its original meaning. Eventually it was handed on by Judah to the whole federation of Israel, and passed into the common stock of the nation's traditions about its past.[39] This development must have taken place at a time when Judah's prestige was at its height, and when the links between Judah and Israel were at their strongest. This points us inescapably to the age of the Davidic-Solomonic empire. This fact, viewed in the light of a number of important historical and religious considerations, leads us to see a significant connection between the figures of Abraham and David.

[39] This position is accepted by A. Alt, *op. cit.*, p. 54.

V

DAVID AND ABRAHAM

WE have argued in the preceding chapter that Abraham was an ancestor of the Judahite tribal union, and that the tradition which told how the ancient god of Mamre had made a covenant with him was preserved among its clans. It was through Judah that this tradition passed into the wider custodianship of Israel, and it is not difficult to see that this took place at the time when a strong political union was achieved between Israel and Judah. The priority given to Abraham as the great ancestor of all Israel reflects the position of pre-eminence which was claimed by Judah at this time. It is therefore reasonable to look for connections between David and the tradition concerning Abraham, and to suggest that a number of very important links relate these two great figures to each other. There are several clues which suggest that the tradition of the Abrahamic covenant contributed to David's own religious and political achievements, and that the importance which has been given by the Old Testament sources to the memory of Abraham has been affected by the part which David played in its preservation.

In the first place one of the strongest arguments for recognizing that David was closely associated with the people among whom the Abraham tradition was current is the fact that David's career was closely related to the city of Hebron. David was himself a Judahite from Bethlehem, so that it is in no way surprising that he should have been concerned with the leading city of Judah. At the time when he lived as an outlaw from Saul he married Abigail, the widow of a Calebite.[1] and sought to win the support of the citizens of Hebron, among other cities of Judah, by sending them a part of the spoil which he obtained from his raiding parties.[2]

[1] I Sam. 25.2ff. H. Winckler, *Geschichte Israels in Einzeldarstellungen*, I, Leipzig, 1895, p. 25, makes the intriguing suggestion on the basis of I Sam. 25 that David was a 'prince of Caleb'. He finds this title in II Sam. 3.8, emending *ro'š keleb* to *ro'š kālēb* = prince of Caleb. Cf. also S. Mowinckel, *Donum Natalicium H. S. Nyberg oblatum*, p. 194.   [2] I Sam. 30.26-31.

As M. L. Newman points out,[3] incidental references in the Old
Testament show that during his early career David was connected
with most of the clans and tribes which comprised the Judah
federation. Most significantly, after the death of Saul and Jonathan
in the battle of Mount Gilboa, David moved into Hebron.[4] The
historian particularly points out that David took this action after
having consulted Yahweh, and that the decision to go to Hebron
was made on the basis of divine guidance. The political astuteness
of this move need cast no doubt on the sincerity of David's action
in resorting to the sacred oracle. Once David was established in
Hebron we read: 'And the men of Judah came, and there they
anointed David king over the house of Judah.' (II Sam. 2.4).

This brief notice hides a wealth of historical problems which
call for explanation.[5] The 'men of Judah' must have been the
elders of the various clans which comprised the tribal union
known as 'the house of Judah'. Their need to travel to Hebron
shows that they were not normally resident in the city, and that
they came from the various settlement areas of the clans themselves. We have no knowledge that Judah had ever previously had
any independent kings of its own, although we need not doubt
that Saul's kingship extended over Judah. The action of the men
of Judah in anointing David to be king over them is explicable as
a defensive action by clans which realized that their own security
had been gravely threatened by the death of Saul and the defeat of
Israel.[6] David's kingship was primarily a military leadership given
to him at a time of great crisis.

The question also arises why anointing was accepted as the
necessary rite of installation for kings. There is no doubt that
Saul had been anointed to his royal office over Israel,[7] probably in
Gilgal, although the records of this event have been the subject
of later elaboration.[8] David's particular respect for Saul was based
upon his interpretation of the sacral status conferred by anointing.[9]

[3] M. L. Newman, *The People of the Covenant*, p. 152.
[4] II Sam. 2.1-4.
[5] Cf. A. Alt, 'The Formation of the Israelite State in Palestine', *Essays on
Old Testament History and Religion*, Oxford, 1966, pp. 211ff., who points out
that the origin of the Judahite kingship is obscure.
[6] M. Noth, *The History of Israel*, p. 182, argues that David himself played a
considerable part in persuading the clans to elect him as king.
[7] I Sam. 10.1.
[8] Cf. especially K. D. Schunck *Benjamin* . . ., pp. 126ff.
[9] I Sam. 24.6; 26.9; II Sam. 1.16; cf. 4.9ff.

There are many indications that the use in Israel of a rite of anointing for the installation of kings, which was not widely practised in the ancient Near East, was derived from Egypt.[10] The local kings of cities such as Hebron and Jerusalem, who at one time were Egyptian vassals, would certainly have been anointed as subordinate officials of the Egyptian pharaoh. In Jerusalem it is possible that such pro-Egyptian vassals were still in office in the early days of David's success. There is every likelihood that the rite was adopted by Israel as a traditional symbolic act for installation to kingship from the knowledge of the Egyptian practice. The particular interpretation given to it in Israel may at first have been quite fluid, since in the case of both Saul's and David's election to kingship it did not betoken any vassalage to Egypt.[11] It is quite possible that David interpreted

[10] E. Kutsch, *Salbung als Rechtsakt im Alten Testament und im alten Orient*, (BZAW 87), Berlin, 1963, p. 57.; R. de Vaux, 'Le roi d'Israel, vassal de Yahvé', *Mélanges Eugène Tisserant*, Vol. I, Rome, 1964, pp. 131ff. Cf. also G. von Rad, 'The Royal Ritual of Judah', *The Problem of the Hexateuch and Other Essays*, Edinburgh, 1966, pp. 222-31, who has shown that much of the Judaean royal ritual appears to have been borrowed from earlier Egyptian practice. The main source of this borrowing would seem to have been Jerusalem, where David took over the tradition and authority of the Jebusite kingship. In the act of anointing, however, it is plain that it was adopted by Israel prior to David's capture of Jerusalem. M. Noth, 'Office and Vocation in the Old Testament', *The Laws in the Pentateuch and Other Essays*, Edinburgh, 1966, p. 239, has suggested that Israel's adoption of anointing came from Hittite sources *via* Canaanite mediation. Cf. also M. Vieyra, 'Rites de purification hittites', *RHR* 119, 1939, pp. 137ff.; E. Kutsch, *op. cit.*, p. 56.

[11] R. de Vaux, *Mélanges Eugène Tisserant*, pp. 119ff., argues that the adoption by Israel of a rite of anointing for her kings arose from the interpretation of the Israelite monarch as a vassal of Yahweh. He relates this to the earlier significance of anointing as a rite of vassalage to the Egyptian pharaoh, and also the alleged familiarity of Israel with the form of ancient Near Eastern vassal treaties. Although it is not impossible that the interpretation of the rite of anointing as a sign of vassalage to Yahweh appeared in Israel, it is exceedingly improbable that this can be used to explain Israel's adoption of the rite. At first it must have been a purely historical borrowing of a ceremonial rite, to which more than one interpretation could be attached.

E. Kutsch, *op. cit.*, pp. 55ff., traces two interpretations of the significance of anointing. The earlier view may be described as democratic in which authority was conferred through the rite of anointing by tribal representatives. Thus the ruler received his authority from the people. The later view was sacral and dynastic in character, in which a priest conferred authority from God by means of this rite. From the democratic anointing by Israel's elders (II Sam. 2.4; 5.3), Kutsch traces a change in the interpretation of the rite by the time of Solomon's accession to the throne, where the roles of Zadok as priest and Nathan as prophet (I Kings 1.34) point to authority being conferred by God. The sharp distinction between these views, how-the sacral significance of anointing in a much more serious and significant way than did Saul and his entourage. This may well be explained by the fact that through his contacts in Hebron and the South David was in closer proximity to cities where anointed vassals of the Egyptian pharaoh had once held office than was Saul.

David reigned as king in Hebron for a total of seven and a half years,[12] and for part of this time a rival kingship over Israel existed in the person of Saul's son Ishbaal. With Ishbaal's death the elders of Israel sent emissaries to David in Hebron to make him king over all Israel:

> Then all the tribes of Israel came to David at Hebron, and said, 'Behold we are your bone and flesh. In the past, when Saul was king over us, it was you that led out and brought in Israel; and Yahweh said to you, "You shall act as shepherd over my people Israel, and you shall be commander over Israel." So all the elders of Israel came to the king at Hebron; and king David made a covenant with them in Hebron in Yahweh's presence, and they anointed David king over Israel.' (II Sam. 5.1-3)

The importance of this account is very great since it provides us with a clear testimony to the circumstances of David's exaltation to kingship over all Israel.[13] It presupposes that a relationship already existed between Israel and Judah. The assertion 'We are your bone and flesh' must be regarded as an indication that Israel recognized a political bond which already united the two tribal groups. Also David's previous leadership over the Israelite army is firmly attested. The request that David should serve as king over

---

ever, is rejected by de Vaux (*Mélanges Eugène Tisserant*, p. 133 note), since tribal elders presumably acted through a priest. This is also the view of M. Noth, *The History of Israel*, p. 183 note, who states, 'The "men of Judah" could only proclaim David king, whilst the anointing was no doubt performed by a priest.'

The likelihood is that Israel adopted the rite of anointing from an ancient precedent established at the time of Egyptian sovereignty over Canaan, and that the significance of the act was not uniformly interpreted. In course of time, in the court circle of Jerusalem, a very distinctive theology of the monarchy was established which gave a particular significance to the rite of anointing. Thus the term 'Messiah' came to have a special importance for the king, and subsequently to the figure of the eschatological king.

[12] II Sam. 2.11; 5.5.

[13] Cf. M. Noth, 'God, King and Nation in the Old Testament', *The Laws in the Pentateuch*, p. 164. G. Fohrer, 'Der Vertrag zwischen König und Volk in Israel', *ZAW* 71, 1959, pp. 1ff.

Israel was strengthened by these two affirmations that David, as a Judahite, was already related to Israel, and that he had already provided leadership for her army. Whilst this account recognizes that Israel and Judah were free to act as two separate tribal groups, it also shows that this independence was by no means absolute. Once again the act of installation to kingship took place by a rite of anointing in Hebron, and a covenant was drawn up between David and the leaders of Israel. Since no covenant is mentioned in connection with David's earlier accession to kingship over Judah, it is reasonable to conclude that the purpose of its introduction here was a consequence of the felt differences between Israel and Judah. Israel sought to safeguard its own rights and privileges by defining them clearly, and by requiring the king to recognize them. For his part also David would have needed to know the measure of loyalty and support which Israel would yield to him. There is no reason for accepting that this covenant was in any way related to the Sinai covenant as an extension, or ratification, of it. It was simply an *ad hoc* arrangement concluded between David and Israel which clarified and defined the terms of his leadership.[14]

For the purpose of our study the significant feature is that once again Hebron was the centre from which David negotiated. This was his capital from which he exercised kingship for seven and a half years, and his choice of it must undoubtedly lie in the fact that it was the chief city of Judah. By this close association with Hebron David was brought into a relation with the ancient tradition of Abraham, the ancestor of the Judahite federation.[15] The circumstances arose in which, with David's success against the Philistines and the new eminence that Judah attained, the old promise of land to the patriarch could be regarded as foreshadowing the greatness which Judah was to attain under David. The close geographical link between David and Hebron, and the fact that the shrine of Mamre was the focus of the tradition of the covenant with Abraham, therefore provides a basis for recognizing that a connection was seen in Israel between David and the ancestral figure of Abraham. This opens the way for us to

[14] Cf. M. Noth, *The History of Israel*, pp. 186ff. H. J. Kraus, *Worship in Israel. A Cultic History of the Old Testament*, Oxford, 1966, p. 180. G. Widengren, 'King and Covenant', *JSS* 2, 1957, pp. 1ff.
[15] Cf. A. Alt, *op. cit.*, p. 54 note.

proceed to an investigation of the account of the covenant between Yahweh and David, and to see if there are any connections
between this and the earlier covenant with Abraham.

The kingship which David exercised over Israel was the
beginning of a long period of monarchic rule in which the
principle of dynastic succession was firmly established. David,
unlike Saul, was able to found a dynasty, and although after
Solomon's death the majority of the tribes of Israel seceded from
this dynastic rule, its sovereignty over Judah endured for four
centuries. In later years the memory of this dynastic monarchy
provided a basis for the hope of a coming messianic deliverer. The
strength of this dynastic monarchic claim on the part of David's
family rested on far more than the popular admiration and grati-
tude which was accorded to David himself. It was believed to
have been grounded in a divine covenant which Yahweh had
made with David at the time of his installation as king in Jerusalem, and so to rest upon the divine will for Israel. This covenant,
with its religio-political claims, gave formal expression to the
institution of kingship in Israel, and the lack of any such covenant
for the rulers of the seceding Northern Kingdom has been noted
as a factor contributing to the political instability of that kingdom.[16]

There is no reason to doubt that the belief in a covenant
between Yahweh and David arose very early, probably within
David's lifetime, and certainly no later than the time of Solomon's
reign.[17] It was a piece of court theology which proved to be
eminently successful in establishing the claims of the Davidic
house over Israel. It was celebrated in the Jerusalem cult, and was
fully supported by the Zadokite priesthood of the temple. The
assertions of the divine election of Mount Zion as Yahweh's
dwelling place, and of David's house to provide Israel's kings,
became central features of the religious traditions of Jerusalem.
In spite of this historical importance of the Davidic covenant its
origin is covered in some obscurity, and the source, or sources,
of such a dynastic covenant are far from clear.

The account of the origin of the covenant between Yahweh and

[16] A. Alt, 'The Monarchy in Israel and Judah', *Essays on O.T. History and
Religion*, Oxford, 1966, pp. 246ff.
[17] For the Davidic covenant see my *God and Temple. The Idea of the Divine
Presence in Ancient Israel*, Oxford, 1965, pp. 55ff.

David in II Sam. 7 bears evidence of some later elaboration before attaining its present literary form.[18] From other references which the Deuteronomistic historian makes to the religious responsibilities of the Davidic rulers it is clear that he intended the Davidic covenant to be regarded as a subordinate extension of the earlier covenant made between Yahweh and Israel on Horeb.[19] To some extent this must reflect the actual circumstances of the Davidic covenant in the time of its origin, since David, by his concern for the ark, showed a genuine anxiety to come to terms with the religious and political traditions of the earlier period.[20] The idea of a sacred covenant did not emerge *de novo* in Israel under David, but had of necessity to be related to existing ideas of Israel's relationship to Yahweh. Nevertheless it is not possible to conclude that the Davidic covenant was simply an extension and adaptation of the earlier covenant of Horeb-Sinai. The introduction of a dynastic monarchy by David represented a disturbing and disruptive influence upon the earlier life of the Israelite tribal federation. In particular we must note that the form of the Davidic covenant is very different from the form of the Sinai covenant. The latter is a law covenant made with the entire nation in which Moses acted as mediator, whereas the former is a promissory covenant made between Yahweh and an individual in which the nation was involved as a third party. Moreover, the promissory character of the Davidic covenant is further enhanced and strengthened by the specific assertion that the covenant is to

[18] The original position of II Sam. 7 in an earlier written source is not wholly clear. L. Rost, 'Die Überlieferung von der Thronnachfolge Davids', *Das kleine Credo und andere Studien zum A.T.*, Heidelberg, 1965, pp. 159ff., regarded it as contained within the Succession Document, which narrated how Solomon acceded to the throne. More recently H.-U. Nübel, *Davids Aufstieg in der frühen israelitischer Geschichtschreibung*, Dissertation, Bonn, 1959, pp. 82ff., has claimed that II Sam. 7 forms the climax of the story of David's rise to power. Strong arguments can be made for both positions. A. Weiser, 'Die Tempelbaukrise unter David', *ZAW* 77, 1965, pp. 153-68, has claimed that II Sam. 7 is a unity, deriving in roughly its present form from the Davidic-Solomonic age. It is improbable, however, that the indications of later elaboration, and of Deuteronomistic editing, can be so completely discounted in this way. The most that we can claim is that there is included in II Sam. 7 a very ancient nucleus of tradition, which centres upon vv. 11b and 16.

[19] I Kings 2.1-4; 8.56-61; 11.11; II Kings 17.7ff.; 18.6, 12; 23.25.

[20] Cf. M. Noth, 'Jerusalem and the Israelite Tradition', *The Laws in the Pentateuch*, pp. 134ff. H. J. Kraus, *Worship in Israel*, pp. 188ff. See further my *Prophecy and Covenant* (SBT 43), London, 1965, pp. 56ff.

remain in force for ever (v. 16). Although obedience to Yahweh is demanded from succeeding generations of Davidic rulers this is not envisaged as jeopardizing the continuance of the covenant. The purpose of referring to the divine chastisement of erring sons (vv. 14-15) is to reinforce the assertion that this will not lead to the annulling of the covenant. Saul's failure to found a dynasty would not be repeated in David's family. In the Sinai covenant the law entered as a demand upon Israel, and so provided a condition of the continuance of the covenant.[21] The possibility that the Sinai covenant could be brought to an end through Israel's disobedience is reflected in the tradition of the wilderness period,[22] and is fundamental to the preaching of such prophets as Amos and Hosea.[23]

We must conclude that the Davidic covenant is formally to be distinguished from the type of law covenant found in the Sinai-Horeb tradition. It is impossible to suppose that the former arose out of the latter through a process of natural development. The type of promissory covenant which we find recorded in II Sam. 7 must have been introduced into Israel from another source. At this point we can consider the importance of the fact that this type of covenant is precisely that which we have found to be reflected in Genesis 15 as the original nucleus of the Abrahamic covenant. In view of our argument for the antiquity of this covenant, and in agreement with the close links which bound David to Hebron where the Abrahamic covenant tradition was located, we may reasonably conclude that the form of the Davidic covenant was influenced by the recollection in Jerusalem of the ancient covenant with Abraham. This is the position advocated by G. E. Mendenhall,[24] and with it we substantially agree. At the same time it is probably too simple an explanation of the historical facts to accept that the Davidic covenant was fashioned in Israel solely

---

[21] M. L. Newman, *The People of the Covenant*, argues that the Northern (E) tradition of the Sinai covenant had a conditional character, whilst that of the South (J) stressed its permanent validity. See esp. pp. 34, 37f., 149, 175.

[22] Ex. 32.31ff. E; Num. 14.11ff. JE.

[23] Cf. especially W. Zimmerli, *The Law and the Prophets. A Study of the Meaning of the Old Testament*, Oxford, 1965, pp. 61ff., and my *Prophecy and Covenant*, pp. 76ff.

[24] G. E. Mendenhall, *BA* 17, p. 72, 'The tradition of the covenant with Abraham became the pattern of a covenant between Yahweh and David. . . . The covenant with Abraham was the "prophecy" and that with David the "fulfilment".' Cf. D. N. Freedman, *Interpretation* 18, p. 427.

on the basis of the older Abrahamic covenant. A number of considerations urge us to caution.

In the first place we must bear in mind that our earliest written account of the Abrahamic covenant stems from the post-Davidic age. It is perfectly possible that the Yahwist's account of the covenant with Abraham in Genesis 15 has itself been moulded by the form of the covenant between Yahweh and David as part of a conscious attempt to relate the two.[25] Secondly we have already noted that there are traces in Genesis 15 of royal motifs which suggest that Genesis 15 has been influenced by the Jerusalem court theology. Thirdly we must accept that it is antecedently probable that the royal covenant of II Sam. 7 was influenced in its origin by other Near Eastern conceptions of kingship, especially that which was current in the Canaanite city states. It is a false contrast to set Israel's idea of the divine election of its kings too sharply against the elaborate court style of the ancient Near East, since the idea of the divine election of kings was current in the ancient world,[26] and the dynastic covenant of II Sam. 7 shows us the distinctive form which this belief in royal election took in Israel. It is probable, therefore, that the Davidic covenant was influenced by current conceptions of kingship in the ancient world, and was not simply an Israelite formulation based on the tradition of the older Abrahamic covenant. We must recognize consequently that the account in Genesis 15 of the Abrahamic covenant has been influenced in its formulation by features drawn from the Davidic covenant of Jerusalem. This does not preclude, however, that we should also recognize that the latter covenant was indebted for its origin to certain features belonging to the tradition of the Abrahamic covenant of Mamre. The fact that this influence was important has led to a conscious assimilation of the form of the two covenants to each other in their respective written accounts. This further strengthens our main contention that there was a close connection, both in historical significance and religious interpretation, between the Abrahamic and the Davidic covenants.

[25] So A. Caquot, *Semitica* 12, pp. 62ff., who argues that Gen. 15 originated from the Jerusalem court circle in the post-Davidic age. Cf. also R. A. Carlson, *David, the Chosen King. A Traditio-Historical Approach to the Second Book of Samuel*, Uppsala, 1964, pp. 115f., and D. J. McCarthy, 'Covenant in the Old Testament. The Present State of Inquiry', *CBQ* 27, 1965, p. 236 note.

[26] H. Frankfort, *Kingship and the Gods. A Study of Ancient Near Eastern Religion as the Integration of Society and Nature*, Chicago, 1948, pp. 238ff.

This connection was not simply that the older covenant influenced the later at the time of its institution, but that the later covenant continued to influence the tradition of the earlier. Thus we may establish that there was a material connection between the tradition of Abraham and the rise of David, and the fortunes of the Davidic house greatly affected the significance that was attached in Israel to the ancient covenant with Abraham.

In seeking to establish the various influences which contributed to the formulation of the Davidic covenant we must recognize the complexity of the traditions, both political and religious, which affected Israel during the Davidic-Solomonic era. The older traditions of the Israelite tribal federation, with its special interest in the ancient covenant of Sinai, were factors of very real significance, and David's acceptance of them is fully evidenced by his exceptional concern for the ark. At the same time we have also noted the distinctive Southern traditions of Hebron, where David himself had risen to power, and which contributed greatly to the political and religious thinking of the king. Further to these influences we must give due weight to the fact that, although a dynastic monarchy was an innovation in Israel, it was an ancient institution in the city kingdoms of Canaan which David took over. Most of all we know that there was an ancient Jebusite kingship in Jerusalem, of the order of Melchizedek, and under the patronage of the deity El-'Elyon.[27] It is impossible to suppose that this Canaanite tradition of kingship was not without considerable influence upon the nature of this institution as it developed in Israel under David. To ascertain the varying degrees of influence upon the Davidic-Solomonic court made by these different traditions is now an impossible task. Their presence in the development of the Israelite state, and their effect upon its religion have been widely recognized by scholars. Our present concern is simply to re-iterate this, and to stress that the ancient Judahite traditions of Hebron were themselves of considerable importance, and that it was as a part of these Southern traditions that the figure of Abraham was introduced into the ancestral sagas of Israel. Probably whilst David was still at Hebron members of his entourage associated his greatness with the ancient tradition of Abraham, and linked the two figures together under a scheme of promise and fulfilment. This theme of promise and fulfilment was

[27] Cf. my *God and Temple*, pp. 43ff.

to provide a basic motif for the great epic history of Israel's origins which was composed by the Yahwist early in Solomon's reign.

We have already noted something of the basic outline of the Yahwist's history, and it is now opportune to consider this work again in connection with our major thesis that there was a connection, both historical and theological, between the Abrahamic and the Davidic covenants.

We have seen that the Yahwist created his epic under the theological scheme of a divine promise leading up to a historical fulfilment. The promise was a threefold one, initially made to Abraham and reiterated to the succeeding patriarchs, concerning the possession by Abraham's descendants of the land of Canaan, their growth into a great nation, and their becoming a blessing to the nations of the earth (or 'land').[28] Thus the basic theme of the Yahwist's history is given in Gen. 12.1-3 which forms his introduction to the patriarchal period.[29] Although this scheme is the work of the Yahwist himself, it did not arise entirely as a free creation, but represents an elaboration of traditions already present in the older tribal sagas and legends of Israel.[30] The primary theme was undoubtedly that of possession of the land, which belonged to the very foundation of the whole patriarchal tradition on account of the part played by the patriarchs in leading settlements of Hebrew clans into Canaan. We have noted that this theme was fundamental to the origin of the Abrahamic covenant in Mamre. It is intelligible, therefore, that the tradition of the Abrahamic covenant should have provided the Yahwist with the central theme of his work. In comparison with it the Sinai covenant is given only a relatively minor role. The two are related to each other in that it is only after the Exodus and Sinai events that the promise of the land to Abraham reached its fulfilment.

The original local reference of the Abrahamic covenant to the region of Hebron-Mamre was extended by the Yahwist to cover the ideal limits of the Israelite state as they were conceived in the Davidic-Solomonic age. The promise of the land was made to point forward to the conquest under Joshua, and beyond this to its effectual conclusion in the rise of the Davidic state.[31] Similarly

[28] The Hebrew word *'ereṣ* covers a wider range of meaning than the English 'earth', and could have both a local, as well as a universal, significance.
[29] Cf. especially H. W. Wolff, *Interpretation* 20, pp. 137ff.
[30] Cf. G. von Rad, *The Problem of the Hexateuch and Other Essays*, p. 61.
[31] See above, page 16.

the growth of Abraham's descendants into a nation points to a fulfilment in the Davidic age when Israel became a territorial state and took its place among the nations of the world. Although the Yahwist did not continue his story up to David's time it is clear that this was the age which formed his own contemporary background, and there is no doubt that he was writing with a very positive interest in the new political situation which had arisen in his own day. The fulfilment to which the Yahwist directs the attention of his readers in his account of the divine promises reached beyond the events of the Exodus and the conquest under Joshua to the founding of the Israelite state under David.[32]

In accordance with this it is not surprising to find that the Yahwist has introduced into his history quite specific predictions of the rise of the Davidic monarchy from Judah.[33] The distinctive presentation of these oracles predicting the rise of the Davidic kingship shows that the author attached very great weight to them. Although they were developed from very ancient material, they were *vaticinia ex eventu* in the significance that the Yahwist attached to them. They affirmed the divine origin of the Davidic monarchy from the tribe of Judah.

Besides these specific predictions of the rise of the Israelite kingship there are other indications that the Yahwist was very conscious of the existence of Israel as a monarchic state, and was concerned to show the divine providence which had overruled in history to bring this into existence.[34] His message is an assertion that this state had divine foundations, and was the outcome of a unique divine purpose being accomplished in Israel's history.

It is also by recognizing the political situation of the Davidic state as the background to the Yahwist's work that we gain an insight into the significance of the third of the great *tria* of promises. Through the descendants of Abraham the nations of the earth would acquire blessing for themselves.[35] This must certainly be a pointer to the political situation in which, under David,

---

[32] Cf. G. von Rad, *The Problem of the Hexateuch and Other Essays*, p. 72, who states that the Yahwist's work 'is much more directly related to David than has hitherto been supposed'. S. Mowinckel, *Erwägungen zur Pentateuch Quellenfrage*, Oslo, 1964, p. 55, calls the Yahwist's epic a *Hofhistoriograph*.

[33] Gen. 49.10; Num. 24.17-19. Cf. S. Mowinckel, *Erwägungen zur Pentateuch Quellenfrage*, pp. 56, 126.

[34] Gen. 12.1-4a; 13.17; 15.18-21; 22.17; 26.4; 28.14; Ex. 23.31; Num. 24.7f.

[35] Gen. 12.3; 22.18; 26.4; 28.14.

Israel exercised hegemony over a number of surrounding vassal states. Through his anointed king Yahweh exercised his dominion over the nations of the earth, communicating his blessing to them through his people Israel. Thus this promise found its fulfilment in the birth of the Israelite empire, and it provided an interpretation of the political situation in which Israel enforced its rule over the surrounding vassal states, claiming to confer the benefits of its own divine blessedness upon them. It is clear that the Davidic court contributed to the emergence of a more universalist outlook in Israel, with a claim to Israel's unique status, and the belief that through it Yahweh exercised his rule over the nations.[36] It is this belief that comes to expression in the third of the promises to Abraham.

At the centre of Israel's political power stood the Davidic king, as a source through which Yahweh's blessing and life was conferred upon the nation, and so to all the nations that were allied to it. It is not unimportant, therefore, that one of Israel's royal psalms gives voice to the hope that the Davidic king will become a symbol of blessing to the nations:

> May his name resound for ever;
> his reputation flourish[37] under the sun.
> May men bless themselves by him,
> all nations pronounce him blessed. (Ps. 72.17)

This echoes very closely the language of the third of the divine promises by which the Yahwist historian interpreted Israel's rise to nationhood. Here too then we are pointed towards the situation of the Israelite empire under David for an elucidation of the purpose of the Yahwist. This author intentionally related the patriarchal age to that of the Davidic-Solomonic empire under the scheme of promise and fulfilment in order to show the religious significance and sacred authority of the Davidic state, and to emphasize the grace of God which had brought it into existence. What Yahweh had first promised to Abraham, and reaffirmed to succeeding patriarchs, had been brought to marvellous fruition with the emergence of the Israelite state under David. It is impossible to avoid the conclusion that the Yahwist himself saw an important connection between Abraham and David.

In view of this far-reaching interest shown by the Yahwist in

---

[36] Cf. P. Altmann, *Erwählungstheologie und Universalismus im Alten Testament*, (BZAW 92), Berlin, 1964, pp. 9ff.   [37] Cf. the LXX διαμενεῖ.

the Davidic state, and his conscious attempt to show that the
political situation of his own day had been foretold by Yahweh
to Abraham, we are led to conclude that the Yahwist intended his
account of the Abrahamic covenant to point forward to that
between Yahweh and David. We have already seen that this is
corroborated by the similarity of form of the two covenants, and
by the probability that the tradition, drawn from Mamre, of the
Abrahamic covenant had influenced the formulation of the belief
in Yahweh's covenant with the Davidic dynasty. Abraham and
David were figures which bore a historical relationship to each
other, even though they were separated by a long interval of
time. Of importance for the development of the Israelite religion
is the fact that the existence of the Davidic covenant lent a new
interest and significance to the ancient tradition of the covenant
with Abraham. As it was interpreted in relation to the monarchi-
cal state of Israel, this latter covenant took on a new meaning and
gained a lasting place in Israel's recollections of its divine origin.

We may conclude from the foregoing analysis that it was in the
Jerusalem court that the tradition of the Abrahamic covenant was
especially remembered in Israel. Its old cultic and social significance had passed away by the time that the Yahwist came to write
of it, and, with David's removal of his court from Hebron to
Jerusalem, its old local connection was severed. For the Yahwist
the importance of the ancient covenant with Abraham was to be
found in its foretelling the rise of the Davidic state and kingship,
and no longer in the ancient cultic and territorial claims which it
had once upheld. Thus it was through the Yahwist's relating of
the Abrahamic covenant to the royal grandeur of David, and to
the extensive political claims of his court, that it came to be given
a unique significance for later generations of Israelites and Jews.

VI

THE ABRAHAMIC COVENANT IN ISRAELITE TRADITION

IN Israel's classical prophets of the pre-exilic period there is a remarkable lack of reference to the Abrahamic covenant as constitutive of the divine bond between Yahweh and his people; nor is there any appeal to Abraham as the patriarch to whom Israel's election was first revealed.[1] For the great prophets of this period the election of Israel was centred primarily upon the event of the Exodus, with which we must connect the Sinai covenant,[2] and in the Judahite prophets Isaiah and Micah upon the election of Mount Zion as Yahweh's dwelling place, and of the Davidic dynasty to rule over Israel. We must conclude from this evidence that during this time, in the kingdoms of both Israel and Judah, the Abrahamic covenant was not generally acknowledged as an independent tradition which declared and guaranteed Israel's election. The recognition of this fact, and a consideration of its importance, was very plainly set out by K. Galling in 1928.[3] Although, however, the early prophets display this surprising silence about the Abrahamic covenant and its significance for Israel's election, we have strong evidence in the Yahwist's history that a very high estimate of it was current in Israel at a very early period. If we date the Yahwist's work in the tenth century BC, then there is no obvious historical reason why even the first of the great prophets of Israel should not have been familiar with the recollection of the ancient ancestral covenant with Abraham. How then are we to explain this silence?

I have suggested earlier that at least part of the explanation for the passing over of the Abrahamic covenant by the pre-exilic

---

[1] Abraham is mentioned twice in the pre-exilic prophets in Isa. 29.22 and Micah 7.20. The latter is certainly a late exilic, or post-exilic, addition, and the former may well be post-Isaianic.

[2] Cf. my *Prophecy and Covenant*, pp. 45ff., and see also H. B. Huffmon, 'The Exodus, Sinai and the Credo', *CBQ* 27, 1965, pp. 101-13.

[3] K. Galling, *Die Erwählungstraditionen Israels*, pp. 4ff.

prophets must lie in the fact that this tradition was no longer a current feature of the worship of any particular one of Israel's great shrines.[4] It was a tradition which belonged to the pre-Israelite period of Hebrew settlements in Canaan, and, although it continued to possess a historical significance for Israel, it was no longer publicly recalled and proclaimed in Israel's cultic life. When it was taken up and adopted by the Yahwist in his epic work the tradition of the Abrahamic covenant was severed from its earlier and original setting in the cult.

We are now able to pursue this investigation further and to recognize other important factors which contributed to the history of the Abrahamic covenant tradition in Israel. The fact that the original location of this tradition was in the sanctuary of Mamre serves to clarify the history of its development. When David shifted his capital from Hebron to Jerusalem the status of the new religious and political centre must have induced a very natural reduction in the importance attached to Hebron and its historic shrine at Mamre. This is fully borne out by the comparatively slight part played by Hebron in Israel after the rise of Jerusalem,[5] which contrasts very markedly with its great importance for previous generations. At the same time the application of the promises of the Abrahamic covenant to the situation of the Davidic empire broke completely the original local reference of this covenant. As we have seen, by the time David assumed the crown of Israel the political situation in the vicinity of Hebron had changed so much that the original political and religious claims upheld by the Abrahamic covenant had become obsolete. The tradition of this covenant would not have lived on at all had it not been for the skilful and remarkable way in which it was applied to the new situation which emerged under David. During the period of the monarchy, therefore, the place in which the tradition of the patriarchal covenant with Abraham was remembered was no longer Hebron, nor any other of the major sanctuaries of Israel, but the Jerusalem court. No doubt the royal rituals of the Jerusalem temple made references to Abraham, but essentially the Abrahamic covenant tradition had been severed

---

[4] Clements, *Prophecy and Covenant*, p. 67.
[5] Hebron became the headquarters of Absalom's unsuccessful revolt (II Sam. 15.7-10), and was designated as a Levitical city and a city of refuge (Josh. 20.7; 21.10-13; I Chron. 6.57).

from its original cultic setting with its application to the political situation of the Davidic empire.

We are now able to recognize another important factor in explanation of the silence of the pre-exilic prophets regarding the Abrahamic covenant. By its application to the royal covenant of the Davidic house it came to be subsumed within it. Those prophets who made a strong appeal to the divine election of the Davidic house as a basis for Israel's privileged position under Yahweh had no need to appeal behind this to the covenant with Abraham. During the period when the Davidic monarchy reigned in Jerusalem there was no reason why a prophet should make any independent appeal to the Abrahamic covenant as the guarantee of Israel's election since this election was believed to be assured by the continued occupation of the throne of Jerusalem by a descendant of David. When we recognize the close historical and religious links between the Davidic and the Abrahamic covenants we are able to see that the significance of the latter was implied by the existence of the former. The political acceptance of the Davidic covenant rendered superfluous any independent appeal to Israel's election on the basis of the promises made to Abraham. It was not until the continuance of the Davidic monarch was placed in doubt through Judah's political misfortunes that the occasion arose for a renewed emphasis upon the divine promises made in the ancient covenant with Abraham. This situation occurred first with the threat from Assyria in the eighth century, and then with the rise of the neo-Babylonian empire, resulting eventually in the destruction of Jerusalem. During the period in which the Davidic monarchy was firmly established in Jerusalem there was no necessity to appeal behind the Davidic covenant to that with Abraham, since the latter was regarded as a foretelling of the former.

With this explanation of the silence of the pre-exilic prophets concerning the covenant with Abraham we must turn to inquire whether the pre-exilic cult was equally as silent about it. On this matter we are again struck by the paucity of references to Abraham in the Psalms, in only two of which is he mentioned. From the results of our study so far it is apparent that the sanctuary where we might reasonably have expected to find references to Abraham in the cult was the temple of Jerusalem. Psalm 105, however, where the Abrahamic covenant is referred to as a part of Israel's sacred history,[6] is certainly a post-exilic composition, since its treatment of this covenant shows dependence on the interpretations both of Deuteronomy and the Priestly document. It cannot therefore be used as evidence for the content of the Jerusalem liturgy during the period of the monarchy. The other reference in the Psalter to Abraham is in Ps. 47.10 (EVV.9), and is full of interest since this Psalm is certainly of pre-exilic date. It is an enthronement psalm, composed originally for the Jerusalem Autumn Festival celebrating Yahweh's kingship.[7] Verse 10 (EVV.9) reads:

> The chiefs of the peoples are assembled together
> with[8] the people of the God of Abraham.
> For the rulers (lit. 'shields') of the land belong to God;
> he is greatly exalted. [Ps. 47.10 (EVV.9)]

In the great cultic congregation of the Jerusalem temple there were present representatives of the nations bordering Israel. The origin of this international representation must certainly be traced back to the political situation of the Davidic empire. In this psalm the princes, or rulers, of the nations are described as shields, the warrior's emblem signifying the holder's rank and authority.[9] The reference to the God of Abraham must certainly be intended as a title of Yahweh, and its appearance in this psalm is no doubt due to the importance ascribed to Abraham in the royal court traditions of Jerusalem. Thus although this reference is quite isolated in the language of the Psalter, it may serve to corroborate our claim that during the period of the monarchy the preservation of the tradition of the Abrahamic covenant took place in the Davidic court circle.

During this period the most distinctive development which took place in the history of this tradition is to be found in the book of Deuteronomy.[10] Especially in the hortatory introduction

[6] Ps. 105.6, 8ff. (= I Chron. 16.13, 15ff.); Ps. 105.42.

[7] Cf. the interpretations of S. Mowinckel, *The Psalms in Israel's Worship*, I, Oxford, 1962, pp. 121f., 171, J. Muilenburg, 'Psalm 47', *JBL* 63, 1944, pp. 235ff. A. Caquot, 'Le psaume 47 et la royauté de Yahwé', *RHPR* 39, 1959, pp. 311-37. H. J. Kraus, *Psalmen* (BKAT), I, Neukirchen, 1960, pp. 348ff., suggests, however, a possible dependence of this psalm on Deutero-Isaiah.

[8] Reading with LXX and Syr.

[9] Cf. Pss. 84.10 (9); 89.9 (8), and see above, page 17. The LXX and Syr. accurately interpret the metaphor, and there is no reason for believing that they had any variant reading, or that any emendation is necessary.

[10] For the significance of the covenant idea in Deuteronomy see J. J. P. Valeton, 'Das Wort בְּרִית in den jehovistischen und deuteronomischen

to the Code we find a very considerable emphasis upon this covenant, and its use to provide an affirmation of the divine will in the establishment of Israel at Horeb and in the conquest of Canaan. The interpretative process which was begun by the Yahwist is carried still further so that the Abrahamic covenant gives expression to a theological assertion regarding the divine purpose behind Israel's existence and its tenure of the land of Canaan, stressing that these rest upon revealed promises of God made to Israel's ancestors. The most novel feature in this Deuteronomic interpretation is the severance of the Abrahamic covenant from any direct reference to David, the Davidic dynasty, or even the empire as it came into being under David. A process of 'democratization' has taken place, and the royal motifs which had previously coloured the tradition of this covenant, and to which it was indebted for its continued preservation in Israel, were removed.

No longer is the covenant solely with Abraham, but with all three patriarchs, and it is frequently referred to simply as the oath sworn to Abraham, Isaac and Jacob.[11] The actual word 'covenant' (*berît*) is also used, however,[12] although it is clear that it was considered to consist solely in the word of divine promise by which the land of Canaan was assured to Israel. The promissory form of the ancestral covenant is retained, and the Deuteronomic authors reaffirm its original character by making the possession of the land its primary subject. In the subsequent elaboration in the Deuteronomic speeches of the sacred significance of this land the patriarchal covenant is appealed to in order to emphasize that Israel's entitlement to it is the result of an act of divine grace.

For the Deuteronomists the primary covenant by which Israel lives is the covenant of Horeb, which is made the central focus of the nation's life. The references in the later additions to Deuteronomy to the 'covenant of Moab' [Deut. 28.69 (EVV.29.1); 29.8, 11, 13, 20 (EVV.9, 12, 14, 21)] are certainly to be regarded as the work of a later hand, and did not form a part of the original Deuteronomy.[13] The promissory and provisional character of the

Stücken des Hexateuchs, sowie in den verwandten historischen Büchern', *ZAW* 12, 1892, pp. 236ff. R. Kraetschmar, *Die Bundesvorstellung im A.T. . . .*, pp. 123ff.

[11] Deut. 1.8; 4.31; 6.10; 7.12; 8.18; 9.5; 11.9. Cf. 1.11, 9.27.
[12] Deut. 4.31; 7.12; 8.18.
[13] Cf. G. E. Wright, 'Deuteronomy', *IB*, II, pp. 501f.

patriarchal covenant is particularly stressed where the basis of the Horeb covenant is introduced:

> Yahweh our God made a covenant with us in Horeb.
> Not with our ancestors did Yahweh make this covenant,
> but with us, who are all of us here alive this day. (Deut. 5.2-3)

The significance of this assertion is that the covenant by which Israel lives is that made on Horeb, and the language echoes the liturgy of covenant renewal in which each generation was placed under the obligation to maintain the covenant, and so identified itself with the original group at Horeb.[14] Israel does not live by the covenant made with the patriarchs, but by that established on Horeb. Thus the Deuteronomists repudiated any attempt to set the patriarchal covenant in the forefront of Israel's existence, and very forcibly stressed its subordination to that of Horeb. Yet the two covenants were not unrelated in the Deuteronomic view, for the oath given to Abraham served as a kind of prophetic anticipation of the Horeb covenant, since it was through the latter that the promise of the land was brought to fulfilment. In Deuteronomy it is the Horeb covenant, rather than the Davidic, which forms the fulfilment of the promise to the patriarchs. This is wholly in agreement with the Deuteronomic view of the kingship, which rejected any notion that it was based on a separate covenant made between Yahweh and the founder of the dynasty. Deuteronomy emphatically placed the king under an obligation to maintain the Mosaic covenant.[15]

We can see in Deuteronomy the outworking of a movement towards the definition of a coherent covenant ideology for Israel. The tension between the traditions of the Sinaitic and Davidic covenants had been sharpened by the division of the Davidic empire into two kingdoms after Solomon's death. Deuteronomy reflects the desire for compromise and reform during the seventh century, after much of the Northern Kingdom had been swallowed up by the Assyrian empire, and when Judah was left to reassert the claims of Israel.[16] The source of its knowledge of the Abrahamic covenant was certainly the Yahwist's account, by this time incorporated into the JE historical work. In Deuteronomy the Abrahamic covenant is interpreted as a divine covenant with

---

[14] G. E. Wright, *ibid.*, p. 363.   [15] Deut. 17.18-20.
[16] On the background of Deuteronomy see my article 'Deuteronomy and the Jerusalem Cult Tradition', *VT* 15, 1965, pp. 300-12.

all three patriarchs of Israel, and is made the primary feature of the whole patriarchal tradition. No longer, however, does it point forward to the rise of the Davidic empire, and to the establishing of the monarchy, but to the covenant of Horeb and the subsequent conquest under Joshua. Its royal features have been expunged, and it has become a theological statement, giving voice to the claim that the state of Israel rests upon divine foundations. It is a covenant of election, pointing forward to the future covenant on Mount Horeb. The key to the Deuteronomic view of the patriarchal covenant therefore is that it is promissory and provisional, anticipating the fuller revelation through Moses. In this way the Deuteronomists provided Israel with a unified and unifying doctrine of the covenant by focusing the whole of their interest on the covenant of Horeb, and relating the patriarchal covenant to this.

Of particular interest in this Deuteronomic interpretation of the Abrahamic covenant is that it is made into a kind of prophetic revelation, through Abraham and the other patriarchs, of Yahweh's election of Israel. The promise to the patriarchs becomes a divine oath which is antecedent to Yahweh's acts in history in delivering Israel from Egypt, making a covenant with them on Horeb, and leading them into the land of Canaan. This *heilsgeschichte* is thus foretold in advance, and takes place as a fulfilment of the divine word. Since Deuteronomy particularly threatens Israel with the possibility of expulsion from its land,[17] the possibility is raised that the original fulfilment of Yahweh's oath might be brought to nothing. Does this then cancel the divine promise to the patriarchs? The original book of Deuteronomy does not provide a final solution to what was, from its viewpoint, a purely hypothetical question. It is significant, however, that in recalling the tradition of Israel's murmuring against Moses the lawgiver's intercession makes specific appeal to the patriarchal covenant as the ground of Yahweh's mercy:

And I prayed to Yahweh, and said, 'O Lord Yahweh, do not destroy thy people and thy inheritance which thou hast redeemed through thy greatness, and which thou hast brought out from Egypt with a mighty hand. Remember thy servants, Abraham, Isaac and Jacob; do not regard the obduracy of this people, or their wickedness, or their sin.' (Deut. 9.26-27)

[17] Deut. 4.25ff.; 8.11ff.

We cannot doubt that the reference to the patriarchs implied a recollection of Yahweh's covenant with them, and the suggestion is thereby raised that this was considered immutable, and thus provided a ground of assurance even in the face of Israel's disobedience to the laws of the covenant of Horeb.[18] We have moved some way in the direction of regarding the Abrahamic and the Horeb covenants as expressive respectively of grace and law. This contrast, however, is not sharply drawn, and must not be overpressed. The patriarchal covenant was not altogether without law in that it pointed forward to the revelation on Mount Horeb as the means through which its promises could be fulfilled. Similarly the law given in the Horeb covenant was a gift of grace, intended to enable Israel to live in the land promised to its ancestors. Nevertheless, in view of later developments, it is significant that the oath sworn to the patriarchs could be appealed to in intercession for divine forgiveness after Israel's disobedience to the covenant of Horeb.

In the later introductory section of Deuteronomy, which Wright[19] includes as part of the introduction to the whole Deuteronomistic history, the permanent validity of the patriarchal promise is affirmatively declared:

When you are in trouble, and all these things have happened to you in future days, you will turn in repentance to Yahweh your God and obey his voice. For Yahweh your God is a merciful God; he will not abandon you or destroy you or forget the covenant with your ancestors which he swore to them. (Deut. 4.30-31)

This section must assuredly derive from a time after the disasters of 597 and 586 BC, when Israel's destruction seemed all but accomplished.[20] At this time the tradition of the Abrahamic covenant, by which especially Israel's possession of its land was assured, took on a new significance.[21] A similar appeal to the patriarchal covenant as a ground of hope is found later in the Deuteronomistic history:

Now Hazael king of Syria oppressed Israel all the days of Jehoahaz. But Yahweh was kind to them, and showed mercy to them. He took

[18] On this tension within Israel's covenant traditions cf. D. N. Freedman, *Interpretation* 18, pp. 429ff.

[19] G. E. Wright, 'Deuteronomy', *IB, II*, pp. 316, 351.

[20] M. Noth, *Überlieferungsgeschichtliche Studien*, I, Halle, 1943, p. 91.

[21] In the later additions to Deuteronomy the patriarchal covenant is referred to in a way which shows the great importance attached to it. Deut. 29.13; 30.20; 31.20; 34.4.

notice of them because of his covenant with Abraham, Isaac and Jacob. He was not willing to destroy them or to cast them out from his presence.[22] (II Kings 13.22-23)

The reference to the patriarchal covenant here must be regarded as the work of the Deuteronomistic historian, who has introduced it as an expression of Yahweh's election love and mercy. In spite of Israel's disobedience to his law, together with its moral and religious failure, Yahweh's word to the patriarchs remained as a constant ground of hope. Although this reference is quite isolated in the historical section of the Deuteronomistic history, it shows us one of the ways in which the author of this great historical work sought for a basis of hope and renewal in the dismal situation created by the exile.[23]

It is in the period of the exile that we find a radical new importance attached to the figure of Abraham, and to the tradition of the covenant made with him by God. Indicative of this is the report which was brought to the prophet Ezekiel, whilst exiled in Babylon, of the religious aspirations of those who had remained behind in Judah:

Then the word of Yahweh came to me, saying: 'Son of man, the inhabitants of these ruins in the land of Israel keep on saying, "Although Abraham was only one man he took possession of the land. We are many, and the land is surely given to us for a possession." ' (Ezek. 33.23-24)

These aspirations, which those who remained in Judah after the deportations of 597 and 586 BC clung to, were opposed and condemned by the prophet (Ezek. 33.25-29). They make it clear, however, that in Judah during the exile there was a popular interest in the Abrahamic covenant and a strong appeal to it as the basis for a national hope. It provided the ground for a belief in a future national recovery and restoration. The reasons for this are not difficult to find. We have seen that the original setting of the Abrahamic covenant within Israel's traditions was as a part of

---

[22] The additional words in the Hebrew, *'ad 'attâ* 'up till now', are not found in major LXX manuscripts, and must be omitted as a later gloss by a pious scribe who wished to stress the divine faithfulness.

[23] M. Noth, *Überlieferungsgeschichtliche Studien*, I, pp. 149ff, regards the author of the Deuteronomistic History as possessing no specific hope for Israel's renewal. This is contested by H. W. Wolff, 'Das Kerygma des deuteronomistischen Geschichtswerk', *Ges. Stud. zum A.T.*, Munich, 1964, pp. 308ff.

the religious and political heritage of the Jerusalem court. With
the Deuteronomic movement this tradition was 'democratized',
and given a very much broader reference as a divine revelation of
Israel's election, and as an assurance of its possession of the land of
Canaan. Among the Deuteronomic preachers it is apparent that it
gained a new and popular interest as the divine oath upon which
all of Israel's subsequent history rested. It was the promise to
which Israel's historical existence as a political state served as the
fulfilment. With the deportation into exile of many of Judah's
citizens from their land, and the end of the country's existence as
an independent state, it was natural that the survivors should
have looked back upon the word of divine promise which was
believed to lie behind their national life. What God had first
accomplished through Abraham and his descendants must surely
become a reality once again. The Abrahamic covenant served as a
fixed point, which was believed to guarantee Israel's existence,
and its possession of the land of Canaan. In Ezekiel 33 the prophet
does not refute the popular religious interpretation of the
Abrahamic covenant, but he rejects the claim that those who
remained in the land could be the beneficiaries of it, because of
their moral unworthiness. This popular appeal to the Abrahamic
covenant shows a close similarity to the importance attached to it
in the Deuteronomic and Deuteronomistic interpretations. In
Isa. 41.8 the people of Israel are referred to as 'the offspring of
Abraham', although there is no more explicit definition which
connects this with the Abrahamic covenant.[24]

After the exile, in the great reconstruction of Israel's religious
constitution given in the Priestly document, we find a further
development and reinterpretation of the Abrahamic covenant.
This work, which forms the latest of the major Pentateuchal
sources, endeavoured to provide Israel with a renewed theological
basis for its existence by rewriting the history of its origins. Its
major historical source is the JE history, although an immense
amount of legal and cultic material has been woven into its
narrative sections. As in the Yahwist's history four centuries
previously, the major motif of the whole work is that of the divine
promise, which is anchored in the tradition of the Abrahamic
covenant. This covenant is the bedrock upon which all the subsequent history rests. There are two aspects of its interpretation in

[24] Cf. also Isa. 51.2, 63.16; Jer. 33.26.

the Priestly document which must be noted.[25] The first is that a number of changes have been introduced into the tradition of what this covenant itself asserted, and the second concerns the way in which the Abrahamic covenant was related to other covenants and institutions of Israel.

The Priestly account of the Abrahamic covenant is contained in Gen. 17.1-14, and shows several important developments in comparison with the account in Genesis 15. The theme is once again the divine promise, and its specific declarations centre upon three assurances, continuing the tradition of a *tria* of promises. These three promises, however, are not quite the same as those in the Yahwist's history, and they are now brought directly into the Abrahamic covenant itself. The first asserts that Abraham will become the father of a multitude of nations (vv. 5-6), the second that his descendants will obtain the land of Canaan for an everlasting possession (v. 8), and the third that El-Shaddai, who makes the covenant with Abraham, will be the God of his descendants (v. 8).[26] Thus in the third of the three promises there is a significant departure from the basic promise tradition of the Yahwist's history.

In the terminology of the covenant the most significant new feature in the Priestly account is that God makes with Abraham an 'everlasting covenant' (*bᵉrît 'ôlām*), asserting its permanent validity and its unconditional character.[27] It is noteworthy that this phraseology does not occur in Genesis 15, and that its point of anchorage in Israelite tradition is to be found in the covenant between Yahweh and the house of David.[28] It is very probable, therefore, that it is from the tradition of the royal covenant of the Davidic monarchy that the phrase was introduced into the account of Genesis 17. The failure of the Davidic monarchy, and the

---

[25] For the idea of the covenant in the Priestly document see J. J. P. Valeton, 'Bedeutung und Stellung des Wortes בְּרִית im Priestercodex', *ZAW* 12, 1892, pp. 1-22; R. Kraetschmar, *op. cit.*, pp. 183ff.; W. Zimmerli, 'Sinaibund und Abrahambund', *Gottes Offenbarung. Gesammelte Aufsätze*, Munich, 1963, pp. 205-16.

[26] On the particular significance of this promise see my *God and Temple*, pp. 112f.

[27] This phrase is particularly found in the exilic prophets, where the new situation created by the exile undoubtedly influenced its popularity. See Isa. 55.3; 61.8; Jer. 32.40; 50.5; Ezek. 16.60; 37.26.

[28] Apart from Isa. 55.3, which dates from the exile, the eternal validity of the Davidic covenant is referred to in II Sam. 7.16; 23-5; Pss. 132.12; 89.29; 30, 37 (EVV. 28, 29, 36). Cf. Jer. 33.20ff.

removal of the last of the Davidic kings from the throne of
Jerusalem, had shattered the straightforward political interpretation of the terms of the Davidic covenant as an everlasting
covenant, guaranteeing that David's dynasty would provide the
kings of Israel. In the future the continuing belief in the existence
of such an everlasting covenant between Yahweh and David
could only be justified by the expectation of an eschatological
Messiah, or by the radical reinterpretation of it in terms of the
whole Jewish nation.[29] It is reasonable to conclude that the Priestly
account of the Abrahamic covenant in Genesis 17 has been
influenced by this tradition of the permanent validity of the
Davidic covenant, and that it was the intention of the Priestly
authors to show that the Abrahamic covenant was the basic
covenant of Israel. A further indication that they connected the
kingship with the Abrahamic covenant appears in Gen. 17.6,
where the promise that Abraham would become the father of
many nations is elaborated by the assertion 'and kings shall come
forth from you'. The earlier J account of the covenant made no
specific reference to kings at all, although, as we have seen, it
regarded Abraham as the forerunner of David. It appears that the
Priestly authors were conscious of a connection between the
Abrahamic and the Davidic covenants, and were concerned to
root the whole of Israel's life, including its monarchy, in the
promises made to Abraham.

Another distinctive feature of the Priestly account of the
patriarchal covenant is that it is made by the deity El-Shaddai.
This accords with the carefully presented chronology of the
Priestly document which divided history into a series of dis-
pensations marked by the distinctive use of divine names. From
the age of Abraham to that of Moses God was revealed as El-
Shaddai, and the name Yahweh was first made known to Moses
(Ex. 6.1ff.). There is no doubt that El-Shaddai is a name of genuine
antiquity which was in use in Canaan in patriarchal times, and we
have noted that it may once have had a particular local significance at Hebron, suggesting that El-Shaddai was the original
name of the deity concerned in the covenant with Abraham. It is

[29] Cf. Isa. 55.3, and see O. Eissfeldt, 'The Promises of Grace to David in
Isa. 55.1-5', *Israel's Prophetic Heritage*, ed. B. W. Anderson and W. Harrelson,
London, 1962, pp. 196ff., and O. Kaiser, *Der königliche Knecht. Eine traditions-
geschichtlich-exegetische Studie über die Ebed-Jahwe-Lieder bei Deuterojesaja*,
(FRLANT 70), Göttingen, 1959, pp. 132ff.

not impossible that even after the exile there still existed a living tradition which recalled a close link between Abraham and the use of El-Shaddai as a divine title. This may be related to the suggestion that several features, ultimately deriving from Hebron, have influenced the Priestly document.[30]

Whilst the nature of the evidence renders certainty impossible in these matters it is at least worthy of serious consideration that the Priestly document does provide us with a late testimony to an ancient historical connection between Abraham and El-Shaddai. If we relate this to the close association of Abraham with Hebron, then the suggestion that El-Shaddai was originally the local deity of Mamre gains in plausibility. Beyond this the evidence does not enable us to proceed, and there is no reason to accept that the Priestly account of the covenant with Abraham rests on any other written historical tradition than that provided by the JE history. The importance of the Priestly account lies in its reinterpretation of the earlier narrative.

One other major feature has been introduced by the Priestly authors into their version of the Abrahamic covenant which has had far-reaching consequences. This is its connection with circumcision, which is interpreted as the sign of its institution and validity.[31] This rite of circumcision does not make the covenant conditional in the manner of the law covenant of Sinai, since no difficulty was anticipated in carrying out the requirement to circumcise every male child.[32] It must firmly be stressed that the Priestly authors intended to make circumcision a sign, and not a restrictive condition, of the covenant with Abraham, even though Jewish leaders of a later age may have regarded it differently.

Circumcision was undoubtedly originally a puberty rite,[33] carried out on young males prior to marriage, and there are indications that it was at one time carried out in adolescence in Israel.[34] When it was transferred to infancy we do not know, and

[30] J. Hempel, *Althebräische Literatur und ihr hellenistisch-jüdischen Nachleben,* Potsdam, 1930, p. 152.
[31] Gen. 17.9-14. For the relationship between circumcision and covenant see Ezek. 44.7.
[32] So J. J. P. Valeton, *ZAW* 12, p. 4. Cf. R. Kraetschmar, *op. cit.,* p. 201.
[33] K. Galling, 'Beschneidung', *RGG*[3], I, col. 1091. J. P. Hyatt, 'Circumcision', *IDB*, I, p. 629.
[34] Ex. 4.24-26. Cf. also Gen. 34.13-24 and Josh. 5.2-8, although in both these cases special circumstances are being dealt with. In Gen. 17.25 (P) Ishmael is said to have been circumcised at the age of 13.

it is arguable that this transference occurred during the period of the exile, when circumcision assumed a new importance for those Israelites who were living in Babylon. During the period of the monarchy several of Israel's neighbours had practised circumcision, and although it was not devoid of religious meaning, it was a social rather than a cultic rite. In the exile a number of Israelites found themselves living amongst an alien population which did not practise circumcision, and it became for them a badge of their religious and cultural distinctiveness. It is this new religious significance of circumcision which was reinforced by its introduction into the tradition of the Abrahamic covenant by the Priestly document. As circumcision was the badge of every true member of the community of Israel, so also was that member an heir of the covenant made with Abraham, and a beneficiary of its promises. Circumcision itself was raised to become a token of the covenant, and a reminder of the grace which that covenant affirmed.

In comparing the Priestly account of the Abrahamic covenant with the earlier narrative of Genesis 15 we have noted significant changes. These have largely been directed towards heightening the promissory character of that covenant, by affirming its permanent validity, and by defining the promises which it contained. The process, already marked in Deuteronomy, by which the tradition of the Abrahamic covenant became a theological abstraction is carried still further. Its original historical roots largely disappear, and it is used to provide an affirmation of Israel's election so that it has a purely theological significance, and no longer an institutional one.

A further heightening of the significance of the Abrahamic covenant is evident in the way in which the Priestly authors relate it to the tradition of the Sinai event. This development is wholly consonant with the changes introduced by them into the content of the covenant itself. Following Deuteronomy it is regarded as having been confirmed with the other patriarchs, Isaac and Jacob,[35] and as providing the central theme of the whole patriarchal tradition. Anterior to it we find the Noachic covenant made between God and all mankind.[36] At Sinai the revelation made to Moses is not said to introduce a new covenant, but is presented

---

[35] Cf. Lev. 26.42; Num. 32.11.
[36] Gen. 9.8ff.

rather as the fulfilment of the promises made to Abraham.[37] What took place at Sinai was not another covenant, to which the patriarchal covenant had pointed forward, but the disclosure of those cultic institutions and regulations which made possible the fulfilment of the promises made to Abraham. The basic covenant of Israel was that made with Abraham, and the Priestly authors do not describe the Sinai revelation as another covenant.[38] Since they stress that the covenant made with Abraham is everlasting, and is not subject to any conditional element of law, it is clear that they have set out a conception of Israel's covenant relationship to God which is unbreakable. They view the establishing of the covenant by which Israel lives as a unilateral action of God, revealing and affirming his mercy to all succeeding generations. Israel's election is an act of divine grace which cannot be nullified or frustrated by human disobedience, and it is this election which is guaranteed by the Abrahamic covenant. Thus the significance of the covenant with Abraham is greatly enlarged. No longer is it simply an anticipatory covenant, pointing forward to the future divine action with Moses or David, but it is the foundation stone upon which the whole of Israel's religious and national life is built. It does not promise the making of a subsequent covenant with Israel, but remains in force as the abiding guarantee of Israel's elect status. We have already seen how the way for this interpretation was prepared in Deuteronomy and the Deuteronomistic history.

In the view of the Priestly authors the revelation on Sinai did not introduce a further covenant, superseding the earlier one, but disclosed those cultic arrangements by which the promises made to Abraham could be realized. This must be related to the fact that what the Priestly authors describe as revealed on Sinai took on for

[37] Cf. J. J. P. Valeton, *ZAW* 12, pp. 13f.; R. Kraetschmar, *op. cit.*, pp. 183ff. W. Zimmerli, *Gottes Offenbarung. Gesammelte Aufsätze*, pp. 207ff.

[38] Lev. 26.45 may be an exception to this. Cf. J. J. P. Valeton, *ZAW* 12, p. 2; R. Kraetschmar, *op. cit.*, p. 183, who ascribes the occurrence here to P¹, and K. Galling, *Die Erwählungstraditionen Israels*, p. 35. It is not clear, however, that Lev. 26.45 must refer to the covenant of Sinai, since the context in Lev. 26.42 certainly refers the covenant back to the patriarchs. In the Priestly document the covenant takes on a kind of timeless and abstract quality so that it is possible that we have in Lev. 26.45 a historical foreshortening in which the patriarchs are linked with the generation that was delivered out of Egypt. This is all the more likely in view of the fact that the deliverance from Egypt was regarded as a fulfilment of the promise to the patriarchs.

them a programmatic character, since from their standpoint it provided a historical precedent for Israel's renewal after the exile. Thus Israel stood between the promises made to Abraham and the fulfilment which would come when the Sinai cultic regulations could be carried out. No uncertainty in regard to Israel's obedience to the laws of Sinai could nullify the continuing validity of the Abrahamic covenant, and of Israel's election which this guaranteed. There is therefore in the Priestly document a subtle tension between law and grace which does not deny the significance or reality of either. The tradition of the covenant with Abraham was used to affirm the immutability of the divine grace on which Israel's election rested.

The reason for this particular subordination of the Sinai event to the Abrahamic covenant on the part of the Priestly writers is not hard to find. It lies in the deepened awareness of frustration and failure which had become attached to the Sinai covenant, and which reached its most radical conclusion in the prophecies of Ezekiel. Ezekiel had asserted that no generation of Israelites from the time of Moses had been obedient to the laws of the covenant of Sinai.[39] The curse of the law had fallen upon one generation after another. Both Jeremiah and Ezekiel had foretold that Israel could only keep the law in the future by a transforming act of divine grace in the hearts of its members.[40] Only so could the law cease to be a curse. The Priestly authors circumvented the threat of failure attaching to the Sinai covenant by asserting that the promises declared in the covenant made with Abraham remained permanently in force.

This assertion of the priority of the Abrahamic covenant as the unshakable guarantee of Israel's election is expressed in the Priestly account of the making of the golden calf, thereby following the Deuteronomic tradition of the intercession of Moses. In pleading for the sinful people, Moses makes a special appeal to the promises made to Abraham:

> Remember Abraham, Isaac and Israel, thy servants, To whom thou didst swear by thyself, and didst say to them, 'I will multiply your descendants as the stars of heaven, and all this land which I have promised I will give to your descendants, and they shall inherit it forever.' (Ex. 32.13)

Here, as in the Deuteronomic account of Moses' intercession, the

---

[39] Ezek. 20.1ff. [40] Jer. 31.31ff.; Ezek. 36.26ff.

memory of the patriarchs is appealed to as a ground for God's forgiveness of Israel. In the Priestly account, however, the quotation of the divine promise to Abraham clearly points back to the Abrahamic covenant as the basis of this appeal. Even though Israel should fail to obey the laws of Sinai, God will not forget his promises to the nation's ancestors.

A further emphasis upon the primacy of the patriarchal covenant is given in Lev. 26.40ff., in a concluding section of the Holiness Code, which sets out the blessings and curses which will come upon Israel according as they have been obedient or disobedient to the law. To a description of the curse of banishment from the land, which undoubtedly presupposes the fact of the Babylonian exile, there is added a note on the possibility of Israel's repentance and restoration. The motive for God's continuing mercy and forgiveness is found in the promises of the patriarchal covenant (vv. 42, 44f.). Israel will not be utterly destroyed because God will not break this covenant, nor revoke the promises he has made to the nation's ancestors to give them their land. Once again the immutability of the Abrahamic covenant is appealed to as a guarantee of Israel's continued election in the face of its failure to keep the laws revealed on Sinai. For the Priestly document the patriarchal covenant is the unshakable foundation of the entire religious and national life of Israel. This did not remove the need for a further revelation on Sinai, but it secured the doctrine of Israel's election independently of it.

With the Priestly document we gain an insight into the fresh thinking about Israel's covenant relationship to Yahweh which was taking place in post-exilic Judaism.[41] The new importance that was attached to the Abrahamic covenant derived from the interpretation that had been placed upon it in earlier Israelite tradition as a covenant of promise.

The tradition that the Abrahamic covenant provided a permanent guarantee of Israel's election continued in Judaism, and

[41] For the Abrahamic covenant in post-exilic Judaism see I Chron. 16.16ff.; 29.18; II Chron. 20.7; 30.6; Neh. 9.7; Ps. 105.6ff., 42. In the Chronicler's history there is a demonstrable by-passing of the Sinai covenant in favour of that between Yahweh and David. See A. M. Brunet, 'La théologie du Chroniste. Théocratie et messianisme', *Sacra Pagina*, I, ed. J. Coppens, A. Descamps and E. Massaux, Louvain, 1959, pp. 384-97. For the Davidic covenant in Chronicles see also G. von Rad, *Das Geschichtsbild des chronistischen Werkes* (BWANT IV: 3), Stuttgart, 1930, pp. 119ff.; R. North, 'Theology of the Chronicler', *JBL* 82, 1963, pp. 376ff.

inevitably gave rise to a tension between it and the law covenant of Sinai. The figure of Abraham became expressive of the doctrine of grace on which Israel's election rested, whilst Sinai remained the scene of the revelation of law. Thus, by giving this priority to the Abrahamic covenant, the fact of Israel's election could never become conditional upon obedience to the law.

In a number of respects the Priestly document represents the most profound interpretation of the covenant which the Old Testament contains. It seeks to do fullest justice to the divine grace which underlies Israel's election, and which is the true foundation of its covenant with God, whilst at the same time it recognizes the historical importance of the law as an obligation of the covenant. Its tension between grace and law becomes an aspect of the tension between promise and fulfilment which characterizes Israel's history. Every Jew lived as a child of the promises made to Abraham, and so as a member of the covenant community which was descended from him. He also lived as a servant of the law, who awaited the coming fulfilment when the law would be obeyed, and the divine *eschaton* would break in. The tradition of the Abrahamic covenant therefore had a very important contribution to make to Judaism as an expression of the belief that Israel's election rested upon an act of divine grace, and that the future contingencies of Israel's behaviour could not nullify this initial saving action of God.

VII

THE COVENANT TRADITION IN ISRAEL

In the preceding chapters we have examined the origin and significance of the Abrahamic covenant in Israelite tradition, and we have noted the various developments which the interpretation of this covenant underwent. In the outcome it came to hold a very prominent place in Judaism as a revelation of the divine purpose which guaranteed Israel's election, and which placed this election beyond any uncertainty caused by the obedience, or disobedience, of Jews to the law. The promises of God to Abraham stood as the historical foundation for the belief that every Jew was privileged to possess a unique origin, and would share in a unique destiny, as a member of the people of God. Within the tradition of the Abrahamic covenant, therefore, there were embedded certain very important religious ideas about the nature and destiny of Israel. This religious significance of the covenant with Abraham renders it important to gain as full an understanding as possible of the historical circumstances in which it arose, and to trace the distinctive developments which it underwent.

In the past a number of scholars have argued that in origin the tradition of the Abrahamic covenant was a purely literary and theological construction, which was designed to assert Israel's divine entitlement to possession of the land of Canaan. It was thought to have arisen at a time just prior to the exile, or perhaps even during it, when Israel's continued occupation of its land was placed in jeopardy through the expansion of the Assyrian and Babylonian empires. More recently, however, a rather different, and more historically grounded, interpretation of the origin of the Abrahamic covenant has arisen, which traces its origin to a pre-Mosaic institution of Hebrew clans living in Palestine.

The most important name associated with this attempt to trace an ancient institutional basis behind the tradition of a covenant with Abraham has been that of A. Alt, whose particular hypothesis regarding the religion of Abraham, and of the other Hebrew patriarchs, has gained a wide acceptance, even amongst scholars who have otherwise been very sceptical of his traditio-historical method.

In our own study of Genesis 15 we have accepted the view that its origins go back to pre-Israelite times, but have found its significance to lie in the divine sanction which it provides for the settlement of a Hebrew clan under Abraham in the region of Hebron-Mamre. Its significance as a cult-aetiological legend was not that it described the revelation of a nomadic deity, but that it gave divine approval to Abraham for his settlement in the land. In support of this view we noted several indications that the basis of the patriarchal tradition in the Pentateuch lies in the role played by the patriarchs as leaders of clan settlements in the land of Canaan, and not in their role as founders of distinctive nomadic cults. Thus the patriarchs are to be placed in Canaan itself, and not in the unsettled wilderness land outside it, as implied by Alt's hypothesis.

The tradition of a covenant with Abraham was preserved at the sanctuary of Mamre by the clan, and later clans, who regarded Abraham as their ancestor. These clans were eventually brought together in the tribal union of Judah, and it is the association of the Abrahamic tradition with the city of Hebron and the tribe of Judah which points to a connection between the figures of Abraham and David. Other indications confirm this connection so that we can see in the covenant between Yahweh and David recorded in II Samuel 7 the historical influence of the older covenant with Abraham. Furthermore when the Yahwist historian came to write of Israel's origins he saw in the Abrahamic covenant an expression of the divine providence which pointed forward to the rise of the great Davidic empire. The promises to the patriarch were interpreted as foretelling the rise of the kingdom of Israel, and its possession of the land of Canaan. In this way the Abrahamic covenant came to be incorporated among the traditions preserved by the court circle of Jerusalem.

In later Israelite tradition, as recorded in Deuteronomy and the Priestly document, we find a continuing interest in the Abrahamic covenant as the historical declaration of Israel's elect status, and the foundation of all its subsequent religious and political life. To be a Jew is to be a child of Abraham, and we find in Judaism a very great theological importance attaching to this claim to be a descendant of Abraham, and thereby to share in the privileges of the divine election. That such a claim could lead to spiritual presumption, and to a kind of antinomianism, is evident from the severe challenge which John the Baptist made,[1] and from the emphasis in the Johannine presentation of Jesus's teaching upon the need for Abraham's children to show a conformity with Abraham's conduct.[2] Nevertheless the Abrahamic covenant remained as an expression of the belief that Israel's election was founded upon divine grace, and was not dependent upon the ability of men to secure their election by obedience to the law. In this respect it is significant that Jesus could use the claim of descent from Abraham as an expression of the eternal grace of God towards every Jew, no matter how unworthy.[3]

This examination of the Abrahamic covenant in Israelite tradition enables us to consider some important factors regarding the idea of the covenant in Israel and in Judaism. Most of all it makes it clear that the Old Testament does not contain one uniform doctrine of the covenant, and that neither Israel itself, nor the leaders of Judaism after the exile, reached any single final conclusion as to how Israel's covenant relationship to God was to be interpreted. What we find is a number of covenant doctrines and ideas which are related to each other. Even the fundamental question as to which covenant was the primary institution of Israel's life is not always given the same answer. At the same time, although this variety characterizes the ideas of the covenant which the Old Testament contains, there is also evident a unifying tendency which endeavoured to arrive at some measure of harmony and consistence.

Several scholars have drawn attention to the tension which arose between the Sinaitic and the Davidic covenants in early Israel.[4] These covenants were not entirely unrelated, but they did undoubtedly point to different religious and political traditions within Israel. We have argued in the foregoing study that the Abrahamic covenant did not represent yet another alternative to these two covenants, with independent claims of its own, but formed a part of the historical tradition which belonged to the

---

[1] Matt. 3.9.   [2] John 8.39ff.   [3] Luke 13.16; 19.9.
[4] L. Rost, 'Davidsbund und Sinaibund', *ThLZ* 72, 1947, cols. 129-34; A. H. J. Gunneweg, 'Sinaibund und Davidsbund', *VT* 10, 1960, pp. 335-41; M. Sekine, 'Davidsbund und Sinaibund bei Jeremia', *VT* 9, 1959, pp. 47-57.

royal covenant of the house of David. The need to provide Israel with a unified, and unifying, doctrine of the covenant, which would obviate the earlier political friction and which would establish the true character of Israel as a divine society, is fully evident in the book of Deuteronomy. Here we find a thorough-going attempt to resolve the tensions which had previously existed between the Jerusalem tradition of Yahweh's covenant with the house of David, and the older pre-monarchic emphasis upon the covenant relationship between Israel and Yahweh established on Mount Horeb. Absolute priority is given to this latter covenant as the *fons et origo* of Israel's life. The institution of the kingship is completely subsumed within it, and the patriarchal covenant is regarded as a providential preparation for it. A unified doctrine of the covenant is achieved by setting the Horeb covenant in the forefront of Israel's life.

In the Priestly document of the immediate post-exilic period we find a different attempt to present a unified doctrine of the covenant in which primacy is given to the covenant with Abraham. This is interpreted as a covenant of election in which Israel's future unique relationship to God is foretold and eternally guaranteed. The revelation on Sinai and the institution of the kingship are seen as outworkings of this. A comparison of the Deuteronomic and Priestly interpretations of Israel's covenant basis shows marked differences, even though both of them are attempts to bring unity within the inherited traditions. One of the major reasons for these differences is undoubtedly to be found in the fact that the experience of the exile intervened between their appearance. It is clear, however, that the Old Testament as a whole does not have a single unified doctrine of the covenant. We must recognize the historical differences which at one time existed between the Davidic and the Sinaitic covenants, and note the attempts within Israelite tradition to harmonize them, and to present a fully integrated doctrine of Israel's relationship to Yahweh. The Priestly interpretation, which ascribes a central position to the covenant with Abraham, represents the latest and more elaborate of these covenant theologies.

Of comparable importance to the fact that Israel did not have a single unified doctrine of the covenant is the recognition that the sources of its covenant ideas were also varied. There was no one single source from which Israel drew its conception of the nature and meaning of the covenant. Instead we can detect a variety of sources from which differing contributions were made. Undoubtedly the most important and creative of Israel's ideas of the covenant must be traced back to Kadesh, where, under Moses' leadership, a group of slaves who had escaped out of Egypt came to regard themselves as solemnly bound in covenant with Yahweh. This Kadesh covenant was linked in Israelite tradition with Mount Horeb-Sinai, although it is now difficult to trace in detail the historical and geographical links which brought about this connection. The original form which this covenant took is hidden in some obscurity, and the subsequent written accounts of it have undoubtedly been influenced by later developments. The attempt to trace in the earliest form of the Sinai covenant a basic form derived from international vassal-treaties of the second millennium[5] has been seriously questioned.[6] Although this vassal treaty form did affect Israel's ideas and presentation of the covenant with Yahweh, it is not until the book of Deuteronomy that its influence becomes clearly evident.[7]

The most significant and original of the features which characterized the Sinai covenant was its assertion of a direct covenant relationship between a community of people and Yahweh as its God. Yahweh was not simply a witness to the covenant, but a party to it. This divine-human bond gave to Israel its most distinctive religious belief, and provided the basis of its unique social interest and concern. Outside the Old Testament we have no clear evidence of a treaty between a god and his people.[8] When Israel appeared in Canaan as a federation of tribes the covenant bond with Yahweh provided a religious basis of unity among them, and in the traditions which the Old Testament preserves the

[5] G. E. Mendenhall 'Covenant Forms in Israelite Tradition', *BA* 17, 1954, pp. 50ff. K. Baltzer, *Das Bundesformular* (WMANT 4), Neukirchen, 1960, pp. 19ff. J. A. Thompson, *The Ancient Near Eastern Treaties and the Old Testament*, London, 1964, pp. 9ff. W. Beyerlin, *Origins and History of the Oldest Sinaitic Traditions*, pp. 50ff.

[6] D. J. McCarthy, *Treaty and Covenant. A Study in Form in the Ancient Oriental Documents and in the Old Testament* (Analecta Biblica 21), Rome, 1963, pp. 161ff.; 'Covenant in the Old Testament: The Present State of Inquiry', *CBQ* 27, 1965, pp. 217ff. F. Nötscher, 'Bundesformular und "Amtschimmel". Ein kritischer Überblick', *BZ* 9, 1965, pp. 181-214.

[7] D. J. McCarthy, *Treaty and Covenant . . .*, pp. 109ff.; *CBQ* 27, p. 229. Cf. also his review of D. R. Hillers, *Treaty-Curses and the Old Testament Prophets*, in *CBQ* 27, 1965, pp. 68f.

[8] F. Nötscher, *BZ* 9, pp. 186, 193.

godward aspect of this relationship is always given greatest prominence. Nowhere does the covenant appear simply as an agreement between the various tribes uniting them to each other. The loyalty that the covenant demanded was primarily a loyalty to Yahweh.

The emphasis upon the primary importance of Kadesh and Moses as a source of Israel's particular conception of the covenant must not be taken to imply that this was the only source, or that subsequent covenants were simply extensions of it. In particular we have important evidence of an Israelite covenant at Shechem, which Noth regards as fundamental to the pre-monarchic organization of Israel,[9] and which is reflected in the story of the assembly of Israel under Joshua (Josh. 24).[10] Both Bright[11] and Beyerlin[12] regard this Shechem covenant as primarily an extension of the earlier covenant of Kadesh, widening its scope to include clans and tribes which had not been in Egypt. C. A. Simpson,[13] however, has claimed that Shechem represents the primary source of Israel's conception of the covenant, arguing that this was derived from the Canaanite cult of the god Baal (El)-Berith.[14] Thus on this view Israel's conception of the covenant was fundamentally of Canaanite origin. H. Seebass also has argued that the form of Israel as a covenant community was profoundly influenced by the cult of Baal-Berith of Shechem.[15]

[9] M. Noth, *Das System der Zwölf Stämme Israels*, pp. 65ff.; *Das Buch Josua*[2], Stuttgart, 1953, pp. 135ff.

[10] Cf. on this assembly, besides the work of Noth, G. Schmitt, *Der Landtag von Sichem*, pp. 88; J. L'Hour, 'L'alliance de Sichem', *RB* 69, 1962, pp. 5-36, 161-84, 350-68; C. H. Giblin, 'Structure Patterns in Josh. 24.1-25', *CBQ* 26, 1964, pp. 50-69.

[11] J. Bright, *A History of Israel*, pp. 145ff.; esp. p. 146, 'This was in one sense a new covenant, in that it was made with a new generation, as well as with elements not previously worshippers of Yahweh (Josh. 24.14f.). But it was also a reaffirmation and extension of the covenant made at Sinai, in which Israel's existence was grounded.'

[12] W. Beyerlin, *Origins and History of the Oldest Sinaitic Traditions*, p. 146.

[13] C. A. Simpson, *The Early Traditions of Israel*, Oxford, 1948, p. 648; 'Genesis', *IB*, I, 1952, p. 603. In his introductory section 'The Growth of the Hexateuch' (*IB*, I, pp. 185-200), p. 195, Simpson modified this somewhat by stating that Israel's idea of the covenant 'was at least partly derived from the cult of Baal-Berith at Shechem'. [14] Judg. 8.33; 9.4, 46.

[15] H. Seebass, *Der Erzvater Israel und die Einfuhrung der Jahweverehrung in Kanaan* (BZAW 98), Berlin, 1966, pp. 93f. G. A. Danell, *Studies in the Name Israel in the Old Testament*, Uppsala, 1946, p. 41, also argues that Yahweh was only identified with the God of Israel when the covenant was made at Shechem. G. Schmitt, *op cit.*, pp. 88f., connects the covenant of Shechem

Certainly it is interesting to find a god called Baal-Berith, or El-Berith, at Shechem where Israel itself remembered a particularly important covenant celebration. There are far too many uncertainties, however, for any very convincing conclusions to be drawn from this knowledge. In the first place it is far from clear what the significance of the title Baal-Berith was. Does it mean that the god was a party to a covenant, or simply a witness to it? The latter is most probably the case, since gods appear so frequently in ancient Near Eastern treaty agreements as witnesses who watched over the enforcement of the obligations contracted in covenants, and who punished offending parties.[16] If this was so then the role of Baal-Berith was very different from that of Yahweh in the Israelite covenant, and the argument for a direct borrowing is weakened. The suggestion of R. Kraetschmar[17] is still worth recording that Baal-Berith was the divine witness to a treaty between Shechem and a number of other Canaanite city states.

M. Noth has argued that a pre-Israelite federation of six tribes existed at Shechem, which was converted to Yahwism under Joshua.[18] If we accept that this was so it is still not probable that Baal-Berith was the original god of this federation. It is much more likely that the original deity of the Hebrew federation at Shechem was the El-Elohe-Israel mentioned in Gen. 33.20 (E).[19] We have no justification for identifying this El-Elohe-Israel with

with Baal-Berith, and argues that the vassal treaty form, which he regards as evident in Josh. 24, was derived by Israel from this older covenant tradition.

[16] Cf. F. Nötscher, *BZ* 9, pp. 211ff.

[17] R. Kraetschmar, *op. cit.*, p. 25 note. H. H. Rowley, *From Joseph to Joshua*, pp. 126ff., connects the deity Baal-Berith, or El-Berith, with the covenant referred to in Gen. 34 between Simeon and Levi on the one hand, and Shechem and Hamor on the other.

[18] M. Noth, *Das System der Zwölf Stämme Israels*, p. 76.

[19] Cf. C. Steuernagel, 'Jahwe, der Gott Israels. Eine stil–und religionsgeschichtliche Studie', *J. Wellhausen Festschrift* (BZAW 27), pp. 343f., and R. Smend, *Die Bundesformel* (Theologische Studien 68), Zürich, 1963, pp. 14f. O. Eissfeldt, 'Jakobs Begegnung mit El und Moses Begegnung mit Jahwe', *OLZ* 58, 1963, pp. 330f., also particularly connects the name Israel with Shechem, and postulates on the basis of Gen. 32.28 the merging of a Jacob group with a (Canaanite) group named Israel perhaps one or two centuries before the conquest under Joshua. V. Maag, 'Der Hirte Israels'. pp. 8ff., claims on the basis of Gen. 49.24 that the El-Elohe-Israel of Gen. 33.20 was an old nomadic deity venerated at Shechem whose full title was 'the Shepherd of Israel'.

Baal-Berith, although some connection may have existed. It is impossible therefore to arrive at firm conclusions as to what influence the cult of Baal-Berith at Shechem exerted upon Israel. What remains clear is that covenants of various kinds were known and practised by Canaanites as well as Israelites, and that important developments took place in Shechem in connection with Israel's religious and political structure. It is almost impossible to define these developments precisely because of our ignorance of Israel's life prior to this. It greatly exceeds the evidence, however, to argue that Israel's idea of a divine covenant was derived from the cult of Baal-Berith of Shechem. At the same time we do not need to deny that Israel's understanding of its own covenant relationship to Yahweh was influenced by covenant agreements already existing in Canaan, and that Shechem was an important centre through which this influence reached Israel.

J. Begrich[20] endeavoured to trace in Israel a development in which the older Israelite conception of a covenant as a unilateral gift of grace was changed under Canaanite influence into a contract between two parties. This has been a valuable attempt to explain the different kinds of covenant attested in the Old Testament, but the major conclusion must be regarded as erroneous.[21] We have sought to show in our study that the idea of a divinely given unilateral covenant became most prominent in Israel in connection with the Abrahamic-Davidic traditions. The Sinai-Horeb covenant, with its demands in the form of law, represented a covenant of mutual obligation, though not necessarily implying that the parties were of equal status. We must therefore recognize that various kinds of covenant were current in Israel, and the probability is that this was also the case in Canaanite society.

It was the important contribution of the Abrahamic-Davidic covenant tradition to have brought into Israel a strong emphasis upon a unilateral covenant of election. The sources of this covenant ideology cannot be easily traced, and the evidence points to the bringing together of a number of influences. It was the Yahwist himself who stressed that the Abrahamic covenant was a unilateral gift of God, foretelling the future greatness of Israel.

[20] J. Begrich, 'Berit. Ein Beitrag zur Erfassung einer alttestamentlichen Denkform', *Ges. Stud. zum A.T.*, ed. W. Zimmerli, Munich, 1964, pp. 55ff.
[21] Cf. A. Jepsen, 'Berith. Ein Beitrag zur Theologie der Exilszeit', *Verbannung und Heimkehr* (W. Rudolph Festschrift), ed. A. Kuschke, Tübingen, 1961, pp. 165ff.

Behind his work, however, there lies the Jerusalem court tradition, which was undoubtedly influenced by older Canaanite ideas as well as the ancient recollection of a covenant with Abraham celebrated as Mamre. It is now impossible to unravel completely the various strands of influence which contributed to the formulation of the Davidic covenant, and which were also woven into the account of the covenant with Abraham.

We must understand the significance of the various covenant ideologies in Israel not by theories about their possible sources, but by recognizing the unique way in which Israel shaped them, and the distinctive-religious and political purposes which they were made to serve. The complicated questions of historical origin cannot by themselves explain the distinctiveness of the Israelite conception of a covenant relationship to Yahweh, even though such historical questions are of importance. The way in which an original nucleus of tradition could be developed and reinterpreted must also be given the fullest consideration. It has been the purpose of our present study to show that the pre-Israelite tradition of a covenant with Abraham was of great consequence in helping to shape Israel's understanding of its relationship to God, and that this covenant was eventually set in a position of great prominence. The particular significance which Israelites and Jews found in the Abrahamic covenant is not explicable simply in terms of its original historical meaning, but can only be understood in relation to its later elaboration in connection with the Davidic monarchy. Thus the great interest shown by post-exilic Judaism in the tradition of the ancient covenant of God with Abraham is indirectly a consequence of the impact of the Davidic monarchy upon the Israelite religion.

In closing we may turn our attention briefly to consider the Pauline interpretation of the Abrahamic covenant in the New Testament.[22] The contrast which Paul makes between the covenant of law made on Sinai, and the covenant of promise made to Abraham is not without its antecedents in the Old Testament. We have shown that a very real contrast can be discerned between the Deuteronomic interpretation of Israel's covenant basis, which placed all emphasis upon the covenant of Horeb-Sinai, and the Priestly interpretation which gave primacy to the covenant with Abraham. In particular the Priestly authors stressed the permanent

[22] Esp. Rom. 4.1ff.; Gal. 3.6ff.

validity of the latter. Paul also lays emphasis upon the claim that the institution of the Sinai covenant did not annul the promises made to Abraham.[23] It is clear that Paul was not the first to see a theological contrast between the promises to Abraham and the demands of Sinai, and that he was building upon earlier attempts to resolve the tension between law and grace which had emerged in Judaism. The Abrahamic covenant stood as a witness to the primacy of grace in all God's dealings with his people Israel, and testified to the belief that election was an act of God, and not a state to which men could attain by their obedience to a law. As such it is an important part of the covenant teaching which the Old Testament contains.

[23] Gal. 3.17.

SELECTED BIBLIOGRAPHY

Albright, W. F. 'The Names Shaddai and Abram', *JBL* 54, 1935, pp. 173-204.

Alt, A. 'The God of the Fathers', *Essays on Old Testament History and Religion*, Oxford, 1966, pp. 1-77.
'The Settlement of the Israelites in Palestine', *ibid.*, pp. 133-69.
'The Formation of the Israelite State in Palestine', *ibid.*, pp. 171-237.
'The Monarchy in Israel and Judah', *ibid.*, pp. 239-59.

Andersen, K. T. 'Der Gott meines Vaters', *StTh* 16, 1962, pp. 170-88.

Begrich, J. 'Berit. Ein Beitrag zur Erfassung einer alttestamentlichen Denkform', *Ges. Stud. zum A.T.*, ed. W. Zimmerli, Munich, 1964, pp. 55-66.

Beyerlin, W. *Origins and History of the Oldest Sinaitic Traditions*, Oxford, 1965.

Böhl, F. M. T. 'Das Zeitalter Abrahams', *Der Alte Orient* 29, 1930, pp. 1-56 (rep. in *Opera Minora*, Leiden, 1953, pp. 26-49).

Bright, J. *Early Israel in Recent History Writing* (SBT 19), London, 1956.
A History of Israel, London, 1960.

Brunet, A. M. 'La théologie du Chroniste. Théocratie et messianisme', *Sacra Pagina*, I, ed. J. Coppens, A. Descamps and E. Massaux, Louvain, 1959, pp. 384-97.

Caquot, A. 'L'alliance avec Abram (Genèse 15)', *Semitica* 12, 1962, pp. 51-66.
'Le psaume 47 et la royauté de Yahwé', *RHPR* 39, 1959, pp. 311-37.

Cazelles, H. 'Connexions et structure de Gen. XV', *RB* 69, 1962, pp. 321-49.

Clements, R. E. *Prophecy and Covenant* (SBT 43), London, 1965.
God and Temple. The Idea of the Divine Presence in Ancient Israel, Oxford, 1965.

Cross, F. M. 'Yahweh and the God of the Patriarchs', *HTR* 55, 1962, pp. 225-59.

Driver, S. R. *The Book of Genesis*[12] (WC), London, 1926.

Eichrodt, W. 'Covenant and Law. Thoughts on Recent Discussion', *Interpretation* 20, 1966, pp. 302-21.

Eissfeldt, O. 'El and Yahweh', *JSS* 1, 1956, pp. 25-37.
'Genesis', *IB*, II, pp. 366-80.
'Jahwe, der Gott der Väter', *ThLZ* 88, 1963, cols. 481-90.
'The Promises of Grace to David in Isa. 55.1-5', *Israel's Prophetic*

Heritage (J. Muilenburg Festschrift), ed. B. W. Anderson and W. Harrelson, London, 1962, pp. 196-207.

Elliger, K. 'Hebron', *BHH*, II, cols. 669-70.

'Mamre', *ibid.*, cols., 1135-6.

Freedman, D. N. 'Divine Commitment and Human Obligation. The Covenant Theme', *Interpretation* 18, 1964, pp. 419-31.

Galling, K. *Die Erwählungstraditionen Israels* (BZAW, 48), Giessen, 1928.

'Hebron (und Mamre)', *BRL*, Tübingen, 1937, cols. 275-9.

'Beschneidung', *RGG*³, I, col. 1091.

Gemser, B. *Vragen rondom de patriarchenreligie*, Groningen, 1958.

Gold, V. R. 'Hebron', *IDB*, I, pp. 575-7.

Gordon, C. H. 'The Patriarchal Narratives', *JNES* 12, 1954, pp. 56-59.

Gressmann, H. 'Sage und Geschichte in den Patriarchenerzählungen', *ZAW* 30, 1910, pp. 1-34.

Gunkel, H. *Genesis* (HKAT), Göttingen, 1901, 6. Aufl., 1964.

The Legends of Genesis, Chicago, 1901.

'Abraham', *RGG*², I, 1927, cols. 65-68.

Gunneweg, A. H. J. 'Sinaibund und Davidsbund', *VT* 10, 1960, pp. 335-41.

Haran, M. 'The Religion of the Patriarchs. An Attempt at a Synthesis', *ASTI*, IV, Leiden, 1965, pp. 30-55.

Hoftijzer, J. *Die Verheissungen an die Drei Erzväter*, Leiden, 1956.

Holt, J. M. *The Patriarchs of Israel*, Nashville, 1964.

Huffmon, H. B. 'The Exodus, Sinai and the Credo', *CBQ* 27, 1965, pp. 101-13.

Hyatt, J. P. 'Circumcision', *IDB*, I, pp. 629-31.

Jepsen, A. 'Zur Überlieferung der Vätergestalten', *WZ Leipzig* 3, 1953/4, pp. 265-81.

'Berith. Ein Beitrag zur Theologie der Exilszeit', *Verbannung und Heimkehr. Beiträge zur Geschichte und Theologie Israels im 6. und 5. Jahrhundert v. Chr.* (W. Rudolph Festschrift), ed. A. Kuschke, Tübingen, 1961, pp. 161-79.

Kaiser, O. 'Traditionsgeschichtliche Untersuchung von Genesis 15', *ZAW* 70, 1958, pp. 107-26.

Kapelrud, A. S. 'Hvem var Abraham?', *NTT* 64, 1963, pp. 163-74.

Kraetschmar, R. *Die Bundesvorstellung im Alten Testament in ihrer geschichtlichen Entwickelung*, Marburg, 1896.

Kuschke, A. 'Hebron', *RGG*³, III, p. 110.

Kutsch, E. *Salbung als Rechtsakt im Alten Testament und im alten Orient*, (BZAW 87), Berlin, 1963.

Lindblom, J. 'Theophanies in Holy Places in Hebrew Religion', *HUCA* 32, 1961, pp. 91-106.

Maclaurin, E. C. B. 'Anak/Ἄναξ', *VT* 15, 1965, pp. 468-74.

McCarthy, D. J. 'Covenant in the Old Testament. The Present State of Inquiry', *CBQ* 27, 1965, pp. 217-40.

May, H. G. 'The God of My Father—a Study of Patriarchal Religion', *JBR* 9, 1941, pp. 155-8, 199-200.
'The Patriarchal Idea of God', *JBL* 60, 1941, pp. 113-28.

Mendenhall, G. E. 'Covenant Forms in Israelite Tradition', *BA* 17, 1954, pp. 50-76.
'Covenant', *IDB*, I, pp. 714-23.
'Election', *IDB*, II, pp. 714-23.

Mowinckel, S., 'Kades, Sinai og Jahwe', *Norsk Geografisk Tidskrift* 9, 1942, pp. 1-32.
'The Name of the God of Moses', *HUCA* 32, 1961, pp. 121-33.
'Die Gründung von Hebron', *Donum Natalicium H. S. Nyberg Oblatum*, Uppsala, 1954, pp. 185-94.
Erwägungen zur Pentateuch Quellenfrage, Oslo, 1964.
Tetrateuch—Pentateuch—Hexateuch. Die Berichte über die Landnahme in den Drei altisraelitischen Geschichtswerken (BZAW 90), Berlin, 1964.

Muilenburg, J. 'Psalm 47', *JBL* 63, 1944, pp. 235-56.

Newman, M. L. *The People of the Covenant. A Study of Israel from Moses to the Monarchy*, London, 1965.

Noth, M. *Das System der Zwölf Stämme Israels* (BWANT IV: 1), Stuttgart, 1930.
Überlieferungsgeschichte des Pentateuch, Stuttgart, 1948.
The History of Israel, 2nd. Eng. ed., London, 1960.
Überlieferungsgeschichtliche Studien, I, Halle, 1943.
'David and Israel in II Sam. 7', *The Laws in the Pentateuch and Other Essays*, Edinburgh, 1966, pp. 250-90 'Office and Vocation in the Old Testament', *ibid.*, pp. 229-49. 'God, King and Nation in the Old Testament', *ibid.*, pp. 145-78. 'Old Testament Covenant-Making in the Light of a Text from Mari', *ibid.*, pp. 108-17.

Nötscher, F. 'Bundesformular und "Amtschimmel". Ein kritischer Überblick', *BZ* 9, 1965, pp. 181-214.

Nübel, H.-U. *Davids Aufstieg in der frühen israelitischer Geschichtschreibung*, Diss., Bonn, 1959.

Parrot, A. *Abraham et sons temps* (cahiers d'archéologie biblique 14), Neuchâtel, 1962.

Rad, G. von. *Genesis*, 2nd Eng. ed., London, 1963.
'The Form-Critical Problem of the Hexateuch', *The Problem of the Hexateuch and Other Essays*, Edinburgh, 1966, pp. 1-78.
'Faith Reckoned as Righteousness', *The Problem of the Hexateuch and Other Essays*, pp. 125-30.
'The Royal Ritual of Judah', *The Problem of the Hexateuch and Other Essays*, pp. 222-31.

'History and the Patriarchs', *ET* 72, 1960/61, pp. 213-16.

Robinson, T. H. 'The Origin of the Tribe of Judah', *Amicitiae Corolla* (*J. Rendel Harris Festschrift*), London, 1933, pp. 265-73.

Rost, L. 'Die Überlieferung von der Thronnachfolge Davids', *Das kleine Credo und andere Studien zum A.T.*, Heidelberg, 1965, pp. 119-253.

'Davidsbund und Sinaibund', *ThLZ* 72, 1947, cols. 129-34.

'Die Gottesverehrung der Patriarchen im Lichte der Pentateuchquellen', *SVT* VII, Leiden, 1960, pp. 346-59.

Rowley, H. H. *From Joseph to Joshua*, London, 1950.

Schreiner, J. 'Segen für die Völker in der Verheissung an die Väter', *BZ* 6, 1962, pp. 1-31.

Schunck, K. D. *Benjamin. Untersuchung zur Entstehung und Geschichte eines israelitischen Stammes* (BZAW 86), Berlin, 1963.

Seebass, H. 'Zu Genesis 15', *Wort und Dienst* N.F. 7, 1963, pp. 132-49.

Skinner, J. *Genesis*² (ICC), Edinburgh, 1930.

Snijders, L. A. 'Genesis XV. The Covenant with Abram', *OTS* XII, Leiden, 1958, pp. 261-79.

Tucker, G. M. 'Covenant Forms and Contract Forms', *VT* 16, 1965, pp. 487-503.

Valeton, J. J. P. 'Das Wort בְּרִית in den jehovistischen und deuteronomischen Stücken des Hexateuchs, sowie in den verwandten historischen Büchern', *ZAW* 12, 1892, pp. 224-60.

'Bedeutung und Stellung des Wortes בְּרִית im Priestercodex', *ZAW* 12, 1892, 1-22.

Vaux, R. de. *Ancient Israel. Its Life and Institutions*, Eng. tr., London, 1961.

'Method in the Study of Early Hebrew History', *The Bible in Modern Scholarship*, ed. J. P. Hyatt, Nashville, 1965, pp. 15-29.

'Le roi d'Israel, vassal de Yahvé', *Mélanges Eugène Tisserant*, Vol. I, Rome, 1964, pp. 119-33.

'Mambré', *Supplément au dictionnaire de la Bible*, V, ed. H. Cazelles, Paris, 1957, cols. 753-8.

Vieyra, M. 'Rites de purification Hittites', *RHR* 119, 1939, pp. 121-53.

Weippert, M. 'Erwägungen zur Etymologie des Gottesnamens 'El Šaddaj' *ZDMG* 111, 1961, pp. 42-62.

Weiser, A. 'Abraham', *RGG*³, I, cols. 68-71.

'Der Tempelbaukrise unter David', *ZAW* 77, 1965, pp. 153-68.

Widengren, G. 'King and Covenant', *JSS* 2, 1957, pp. 1-32.

Wolff, H. W. 'The Kerygma of the Yahwist', *Interpretation* 20, 1966, pp. 131-58.

'Das Kerygma des deuteronomistischen Geschichtswerk', *Ges. Stud. zum A.T.*, Munich, 1964, pp. 308-24.

Zimmerli, W. 'Sinaibund und Abrahambund', *Gottes Offenbarung. Gesammelte Aufsätze*, Munich, 1963, pp. 205-16.

'Promise and Fulfilment', *Essays on Old Testament Interpretation*, ed. C. Westermann, London, 1963, pp. 89-122.

INDEX OF AUTHORS

INDEX OF BIBLICAL REFERENCES

OLD TESTAMENT